## WHAT THE MEDIA ARE SAYING:

*"The Wee Mad Road* is a funny, touching, insightful look at the ebb and flow of an isolated Highland fishing and crofting community, a place molded by forces of nature and tempered by its people. Its a road well worth traveling, if only from the comfort of your favorite armchair."

Neill Kennedy Ray, *SCOTTISH LIFE* magazine, Summer 2008

"If you're looking for a respite from politics and war, you can lose yourself in *The Wee Mad Road*...so idyllic it'll make you Highland green with envy"

Mary Ann Grossman, Saint Paul Sunday *PIONEER PRESS*

*"The Wee Mad Road* is kind of like Peter Mayle's *A Year in Provence*, with rotten weather and lots of whisky."

Bob Gilbert, *VILLAGER*

"...a gloriously whimsical account of the Highland lifestyle, beautifully captured in words and illustrations -- the characters, the pub life, the ceilidhs. This is great fun."

Hammish Coghill, *SCOTTISH LIFE* magazine, Autumn 2008

"...a two-year adventure of shearing sheep, learning folk songs and befriending locals. The whole romantic endeavor is captured in *The Wee Mad Road*."

Kerri Westenberg, Minneapolis Sunday *STAR TRIBUNE*

D0051321

# The Wee Mad Road

Cover painting: **Priest Island Sheep** by Barbara Maloney

ISBN-13: 978-1-934690-02-4
ISBN-10: 1-934690-02-3

Printed in the United States of America

First Printing: March 2008

09 08 07 06 05    5 4 3 2

LCCN: 2008925012

Book design by Crystal Nichols, *Arctic Lotus Designs*

Tasora Books
3501 Hwy 100 S.
Ste. 220
Minneapolis, MN 55416

# The Wee Mad Road
## A midlife escape to the Scottish Highlands

by Jack & Barbara Maloney
Illustrations by Barbara Maloney

*"The best roads are the ones that surprise you."*

# Contents

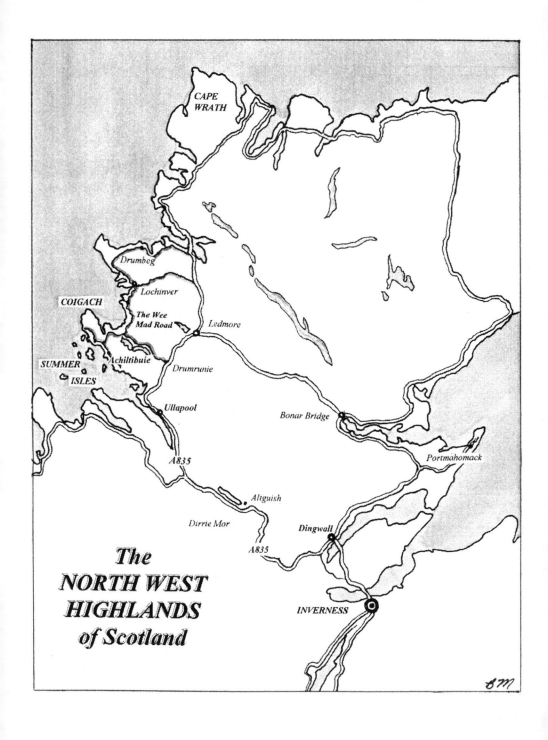

CAPE
WRATH

Drumbeg

COIGACH

Lochinver

The Wee
Mad Road

Ledmore

SUMMER
ISLES

Achiltibuie

Drumrunie

Ullapool

Bonar Bridge

Portmahomack

A835

Altguish

Dirrie Mor

Dingwall

A835

The
NORTH WEST
HIGHLANDS
of Scotland

INVERNESS

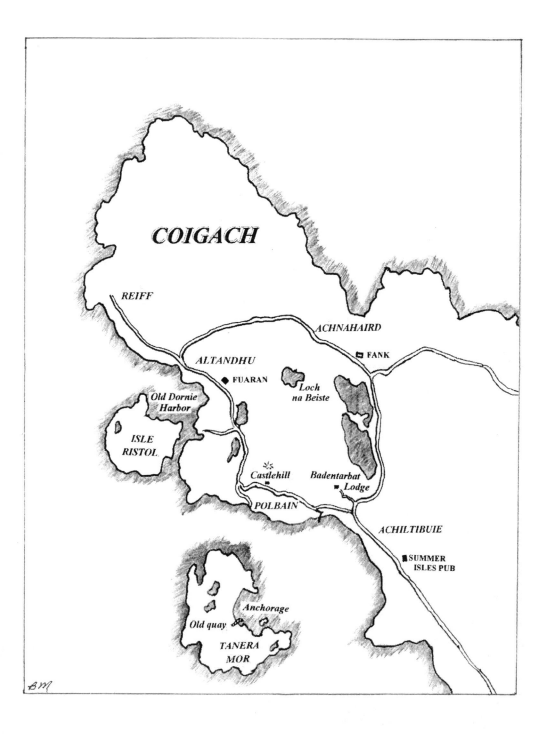

*To all the wee mad roads of life,*
*the travelers who venture on them,*
*and the folks at the end of the road*
*who kindly open their doors and hearts.*

# Foreword

## The Empty Nest

Our children grew up and left home. Before they could come back, we sold the house and ran away to a foreign land.

Okay, there is more to it than that. We were no longer young, but not yet old. The current of our lives, after tumbling along through the rocks and rapids of marriage, home making, child-rearing, and career-building, had carried us suddenly into a still and silent pool. We were in our forties and, for the moment, we were free.

We could look forward to a secure, predictable future, living the same year again and again, each one a little grayer than the last. But turning the calendar isn't a life. Like adult birds when their young fly away, we weren't content to just hang around the empty nest and wonder how the kids were doing. Free at last from the duties of parenthood, birds take flight. So did we.

This book is about two years we spent on the wee mad road between youth and old age. Two years of total freedom to chase our dreams, in a place far from our urban experience, among people strange and familiar, in a world of awesome beauty and isolation. The place was a small village in Coigach, a remote coastal region in the Northwest Highlands of Scotland. The people were shepherds, musicians, lairds, poachers, fishermen, poets, crofters, artists, storytellers, Highlanders and would-be Highlanders. And the world was mountains and valleys, sunlight and storms, rocks and heather and islands in the sea.

# Coigach As It Was

You won't find funny, music-hall Scots brogues in these pages. Coigach is an isolated remnant of the Gaeltacht where Scots Gaelic is still a living language, far from the Lowlands where Robert Burns' quaint vocabulary was shaped. The older people in Coigach grew up with the Celtic language at home and learned their textbook English in school. They spoke in a clear, unsullied and articulate English that left us in awe. Barb and I were the ones with accents – Midwest American accents and speech patterns which must have assaulted the Highland ear in ways I will not attempt to caricature.

We need to make clear that the Coigach we describe here no longer exists, at least in the form that it did when we lived there. Cultural change travels far and fast in this electronic age, and young Scots and Americans today may share with each other more than they share with their parents. We can only tell you what Coigach was like – or seemed like to us – not so many years ago.

Traditional methods of crofting, fishing, and sheep raising were still in use then, though fading, and village life had not yet been dramatically changed by the outside world. Nor had prosperity reached this corner of the Highlands. Most homes were traditional white stone houses with slate roofs, damp and drafty and furnished with spare simplicity. Rusty old cars stood derelict behind croft houses, serving as shelters for the ubiquitous sheep dogs. Fields were defined by ancient drystone walls with makeshift gates, sometimes fashioned from discarded iron bedframes and hinged with marine rope scavenged from the sea. The old men still spoke Gaelic in the blue-smokey pub, and cut and burned peat for their winter comfort, and most of the houses had musical instruments left from the days before radio and television reached them from the Outer Hebrides.

Much of the delight in life there came with music. Folk musicians from other villages, other regions, passed through Coigach frequently. Some came searching for the roots of older songs and airs, some eagerly bringing new ones; all were welcome. With fiddle and guitar, accordion and concertina, pipes, pennywhistle and bodhran, they played and sang for pleasure and drink. And when "Last call" was announced in the pubs, and lights in the Village Hall went dark, the music spilled over into whitewashed homes along the coast, where it was heard through the twilight of midsummer night and on 'til the dawn cuckoo called.

Everyone in Coigach knew I was a writer. Most were afraid I would write about them. Some were afraid I would not. But I was trying to write American fiction at the time, and accounts of our day-to-day adventures in the Highlands were kept close to our hearts, tucked away in private places. Soon they may fade from memory, and with them a way of life that marked us forever. So we'd like you to know what those years were like as we experienced them, through letters home, *italicized entries from Barb's daily journal*, and a few stories about a special place.

# Taking the Road

## To a Friend in America

It was good to hear your voice this morning, even as I stood naked and shivering in the darkness, my sleepy mind groping for words. Phone calls at four a.m. bring me flying out of the cramped little bed and down the unfamiliar twisting stairway before the third ring, for they mean a friend from another world, another time, America. Don't worry about waking us – you're not the first to mix up transatlantic time zones.

Barb came down while we were still talking and put a blanket over my bare shoulders. Drafts whirled through the house, pushed by a gale coming off the sea, and rain hissed and slashed against the windowpanes. Still, the connection wasn't half bad, and I could imagine the room in your house, six hours to the west, the warmth and bright lights of evening. And afterward, when Barb and I went shivering up to bed, we were strangely elated from talking with you, probably the way an astronaut feels when his tiny capsule in darkest space is radio-linked to home.

You asked why we are here, in this old stone house on the hillside above a foreign shore, in a world so far removed from the comfortable urban life we were living when last we saw you. Considering the cost — and the discomfort — of transatlantic phone calls, I told you I'd explain the whole venture in a letter or two. Now, I realize it will take more than that to bring you to the point of understanding. But here we begin.

There's a special place you once told me about. You saw it on a business trip, or a vacation, or maybe it was only in the pages of a magazine; a place that took hold of a corner of your mind. And you said to yourself: one of these days, I'll go there. And stay for a while.

I don't recall exactly where your special place was. Wyoming? Alaska? Africa? No matter. I do remember that it was totally different from the places we have lived all our lives, and that you said it had space and silence and nothing to pull you away from yourself. It was the place your mind escaped to whenever you were trapped in city traffic or stranded at a strange airport or standing in an endless line at the supermarket. Then, for an instant, the clamor of the crowd was suspended, giving way to the rush of the wind and the sea, and your eyes looked beyond the swarming mass to an endless open horizon.

It's a real place, the one in your mind, and you can get there if you really want to. I know that, because Barb and I are there right now. Oh, not in the exact same spot – that's your place, after all – but certainly in the place that is our own.

## The Beginning of the Road

We weren't looking for any special place the first time we came to Coigach. Barb and I were on a three week vacation, threading a cheap rental car down the narrow lanes that weave through the wilds of Scotland's West Highlands. The best roads are the ones that surprise you. That day we had been on many, and we were looking for a place to stop and get our bearings. We turned off onto a dead-end road leading to a busy little fishing port called Lochinver, and stopped for tea at an old Victorian hotel on the waterfront. Beyond the grimy windows of the hotel lounge, we could see steel cranes hovering over a cluttered pier like antic dinosaurs, clawing dripping netfuls of fish from the bowels of sea-stained trawlers, disgorging silver avalanches into waiting trucks. Being landlocked midwesterners, we found it all fascinating — but noisy. We decided to move on.

As we headed back through Lochinver toward the highway, Barb clutched my arm and cried "Wait! Stop! Back up!"

I braked the car. "Not your purse again?"

"No! Back up. I want to look at something. Back up!"

I groped with my left hand for the unfamiliar shift knob, found reverse, and carefully backed along what felt like the wrong side of the road until she said "Stop" again. To our right, a narrow paved track turned off between two trees and disappeared up a hill. At its side was a small, hand-lettered sign: The Wee Mad Road.

"Let's go this way," she said.

"Are you kidding? That looks like a driveway."

"It says road – it's a road."

"It's not on the map — it could go anywhere. Or nowhere."

"Yes. But it looks pretty. Let's do it."

Responding with standard male body language — the shrug, the eye roll that means 'I will indulge your foolish wish but if it goes wrong it's your fault' — I turned the car and headed up the Wee Mad Road.

It was wee, and it was mad. For almost an hour, the one-lane track climbed, twisted, corkscrewed its way between steep heather-grown hillsides, emerged onto a car-width shelf between cliff and sea, disappeared around rocks, scrambled up to mountain passes and plunged into ravines, passing waterfalls and rivers and great yawning valleys where isolated white cottages nestled. Every few hundred yards, the track widened slightly. Protocol on single-track roads dictates that, when two cars meet, the one closest to the passing place pulls — or backs — into it, allowing the other to pass. Thankfully, we met no cars that day, for the passing places were very small, and the drop-offs very large.

Late in the day, the Wee Mad Road brought us into a wide mountain valley, and to a tee intersection with a slightly wider single-track. One faded road sign arrow pointed left, toward the distant two-lane highway and civilization. Another, pointing right, bore one of those intriguing Scots Gaelic names that baffle the eye and the tongue: Achiltibuie.

But the western ocean was in that direction, and the sun was about to set, so we turned and drove out between the hills to a vista that would make a stone weep. Wild fields of heather sweeping down the hills to the verge of a great sea loch. White stone houses scattered like snowflakes above the tide-line. Dark islands beyond, floating on waves of molten gold. Snow-crested blue mountains on the far southern shore. A blood-swollen sun silhouetting the Outer Hebrides on the horizon.

That's how we first came to Coigach.

# Achiltibuie

Achiltibuie is what geographers call a 'linear village.' That is to say, the houses, post office, church, store, school, village hall, hotel and pub are strung like beads along a strand of single-track road hugging the flanks of great hills above Loch Broom. It is a village one house wide, and two miles long.

Beyond the main village, you will find a number of hamlets — smaller linear settlements of white stone houses clustered along the road that traces the coastline — each with its own name: Polbain, Altandhu, Polglass, Reiff, Achnahaird, Achduart. And on and on. Coigach – Scots Gaelic for 'five fields' – encompasses the region around Achiltibuie and its outlying hamlets, including some 200-odd souls. Quite odd, as we have since learned.

As the light was fading, I pulled up at the one small hotel in the main village and Barb went in to see if we could get a room. She came out a few minutes later, with a puzzled expression. "Do I look like a bum?"

"No more than usual. Why?"

"I asked the man about a room and — well, he acted like I didn't qualify for one!"

"What?"

"An Englishman, by his accent — rawther nose-up — you'd think we were asking for a room in Buckingham Palace."

"What did he say?"

"Something about not catering to transients."

"Nice. Very nice. Now what?"

"He did say there might be a B&B down the road that would be willing to take us."

"Eeeew, chawming — thenk yew veddy much!"

I turned our tiny car in front of the hotel, attempting a Parthian wheel spin that was frustrated by the feeble engine. We spluttered out of Achiltibuie, down along a beach festooned with drying fish nets, then up around a headland to where another long chain of whitewashed stone houses was anchored by a road sign. It said: Polbain.

We motored slowly along, peering anxiously until a gate with a B&B sign hove in sight. I waited while Barb descended the path to a nice looking modern house below the road. And waited. Warm evening light washed over white woolly dots grazing the hillside high over the hamlet. Closer, a few sheep wandered along the road, nibbling constantly at grasses. One fed on prickly gorse that would make a goat gag.

Barb returned, smiling. "No room at the inn — but the lady was kind enough to phone a neighbor who has a room for us."

# Wilf and Wendy

The moment they greeted us, we knew the couple who met us at their garden gate weren't Highlanders. They weren't even Scots – Wilf and Wendy had the broad accents of northern England. But they had fallen in love with the Highlands years before, and when Wilf retired from the civil service, they moved to Polbain, fixed up a large old house and took in occasional bed-and-breakfast guests to supplement their income.

Wilf was a big man, spilling over with wit and chatter, his enthusiasm for the country around Achiltibuie boundless. Wendy was small, quick and cheery, a chickadee sort of woman who herded us into their snug sitting room and made fresh tea and scones appear as if by magic.

We told them we only planned to spend the night before driving on down the coast. "Oh, no," Wilf laughed, "you'll need more time here than that!" He spilled an avalanche of maps and folders across the low table, and suggestions cascaded from our eager hosts. "You must go out to the islands on the *Hectoria* and see the seals and sea-birds." "There's wonderful hill-walking, and a lovely craft shop across the road...." "And excellent fishing..." "Would you like to meet our sheep? They're ever so sweet and friendly!"

Our hosts were right. One day wasn't enough. Nor two, nor even three. On that first visit to Coigach, the weather was mostly cold, wet and windy, but it didn't stop us from immersing ourselves in the country. We walked in fine mist to the Falls of Inverkirkaig, clambered in dense fog to the top of The Fiddler mountain, toured offshore in chilly winds on the tour boat *Hectoria*, picnicked in a brief burst of sunshine on the island of Tanera Mor, fished for trout, explored the harbor at Old Dornie, reveled in rain and tides and heart-stopping sunsets.

We stayed at Sea View Cottage in Polbain for five days. Something in the country held us, like no place we had ever been. We both felt it, and to this day we can't explain it. Neither of us has roots in Scotland, much less the Highlands. Yet the wind and the sea and the hills of Coigach played a chord that seemed to sing in our blood. And when we finally had to hurry south to catch our plane home, departure tore at our hearts and tears rolled down our cheeks. "We'll come back," Barb sniffled. All I could manage to say was, "yes." But neither of us could imagine then how soon – or for how long.

# Wishing Time

For the next few years, we kept up a friendly correspondence with Wilf and Wendy, and often our thoughts and conversations returned to Polbain, Achiltibuie and the Coigach region. What a wonderful place it would be to live, if only we could...but it was only a flight of fancy. The practical demands of family and work kept our feet firmly grounded – up to a point.

# Year of Decision

## Fireside Talk

*January 12th*

*For the first time in my life I feel the need to keep a journal. I have reached one of those "passages" in the orderly progression of life – college – marriage – motherhood – career. My girls have grown up and moved out to be on their own. I am 42 years old – 20 or so years from retirement age. Jack & I look at each other and ask "So – what now?"*

What, indeed? One winter's night by the fireside, the conversation turned serious. Barb's job at the art gallery was still fun but no longer challenging. My work as a freelance script writer for small film producers had settled into pleasant routine. Our house had a manageable mortgage and ample equity. Our parents were retired, still healthy, not yet needing special attention. Our girls were gone. In fact, there were no immediate demands on us. None.

We could see a brief opportunity, a year or two when we could make free choices for ourselves alone – and we knew it might never come again. "What about going back to Scotland? Coigach?"

Barb, ever practical: "What would we do there?"

"Live. Enjoy!"

She frowned. "That's not enough."

"Go fishing."

"Oh yeah, right."

"Okay, I'd have time to write. Really write...what I want, not just what my clients want." I groped for a convincing argument. "Maybe a novel I've been thinking about."

"And what would I do?"

"Draw, paint! You love to do that, and you've never had time to work at it."

Snow was falling outside, firelight danced on our faces, the pendulum of the cuckoo clock counted off the passing moments. We were weaving dreams in the shadows.

"What do we live on?"

"This house! We sell it, pay off the mortgage – what's left should support us for a year or two."

"And then what?"

"We'll figure that out when the time comes. Maybe I'll become a famous novelist." Silence. "Anyway, I can always go back to freelancing."

Tick, tock, tick, tock.

"Where would we live?"

"By the sea somewhere. Maybe Wilf and Wendy could help us find a place."

It was a winter evening's fantasy. The next morning, I sent a letter off to our friends in Coigach, outlining our dream before cold reality could return.

## February 16th

*Today we got a marvelous letter from Polbain. Wilf and Wendy were excited by our news and said there are four or five houses on the sea in their area that are for rent and snug enough in winter to suit our needs. They offered to check them out for us, and we can discuss terms with the owners.*

## February 22th

*Our plans move on apace for Scotland. Our real estate agent came over the other night to give us some idea of what we can expect from selling our house. If all goes well, we should be able to live for a year or two on half the proceeds.*

*Meanwhile, I'm still waking up in the middle of the night in a mixed state of panic and excitement, my mind whirling with a million things that need to be done and remembered. I wonder if I'll get a full night's sleep for the next six months.*

# Flitting

There is a surreal scene in Luis Buñuel's classic 1929 film *An Andalusian Dog* in which a man struggles toward his desire – a nude woman. He sweats and strains, but he is held back by ropes dragging a bizarre collection of objects: corks, melons, clergymen bound hand and foot, grand pianos, dead donkeys – all tangling with a clutter of furniture in the room. I began to feel that way in the months following our decision to go to Scotland.

'Flitting' is a Scots term for moving out of a home quickly, possibly one step ahead of the rent collector. But we couldn't just pack up a bag one day and walk out of a life we'd been building for decades. I had months of writing to finish, Barb had a job as well. We had a house and furniture to deal with, and a car and two cats and family and friends and all the detritus of middle class life in the suburbs of Minneapolis. And we didn't know exactly where we'd be going, how long we'd be staying, or even if we'd ever come back.

While I worked on a script, Barb went to Scotland and arranged to rent an old croft house called Castlehill, half a mile up the road from Wilf and Wendy.

## June 3rd

*I am back from Scotland. Castlehill is in such open country – no trees or greenery to speak of. It will be so different! Here in our home garden we have a cultivated, tamed kind of loveliness. There, the beauty is wild and open. Here there is constant noise – highway traffic, kids yelling, dogs barking, construction equipment – along with the sounds of birds singing and wind in the trees. There, there is the bleat of lambs, the robin's whistle, the call of the cuckoo and rush of the sea – not much in the way of man-made noise.*

*I have a much better idea now of the lay of the land, and of the village community. Living there will be an opportunity to experience a whole new way of life – a slower pace, a society much more tied to the land – with a degree of inter-dependence unknown to us.*

*Castlehill, our new home, belongs to Joan & Murdo Macleod*

*– brother & sister – whose family have always been crofters. Murdo is a font of information on the history and geography of the area. Unfortunately he had a stroke several years ago and is quite infirm now. But his mind is still sharp and he and Joan are the dearest people you could ever hope to meet. They are asking very little in rent so we should be able to survive on what we get for the house.*

The final weeks at home were chaotic. Everything we owned had to be stored in a warehouse, or sold, or given away. Ever try to give away two eccentric cats? Much to our relief, an eccentric friend agreed to take them both.

On the last day, we were too tired to feel any emotion as we drove away from the pleasant suburban house where we had raised our children. The house, in the end, was simply a box in which we had made our home. We had emptied that box, and 'home' was now scattered between a storage locker, a faraway cottage, and the luggage riding with us in the car.

## August 25th

*Our last good-byes are said, and we are now cruising at 35,000 feet and bound for London. A friend took us to the airport around 3:30. We had eight pieces of luggage – two duffle bags, two suitcases, a backpack, a garment bag, a wooden crate with my guitar and a few domestic necessities, and Jack's typewriter. The redcap who took our luggage fixed it so that we only had to pay for 1 piece of excess baggage, and not for size overage. He got a generous tip!!*

# Arrival

The pleasant course of our 'flitting' hit a snag at 7:00 a.m. when we landed at London Gatwick. The British consulate in Chicago had given us wrong information about applying for our resident visas. We were stuck in detention for two hours until an immigration officer got around to interviewing us. In the United Kingdom, being 'interviewed' doesn't mean the authorities want your opinion; it is a grilling. The officer questioned us closely about our backgrounds and professions, our finances and intentions, doing her best to find a reason to prevent us from taking up residence. After half an hour of bureaucratic battering, she grudgingly stamped our passports and let us in.

It was late morning before we finally got our rental car loaded and ventured out onto what still seemed the wrong side of the road. We were two city-bred Americans heading for Scotland, Edinburgh, Inverness, the fabled Highlands, and a totally different way of life. But the motorway signs flashing by overhead simply said, "To The North."

## August 28th

*The drive up to Edinburgh was fine – sunny weather and nice roads (only got lost once). Took a nice long walk tonight through the city. There were two girls playing violins in the gardens below Princes Street. An old vagrant wandered up to listen and finally reached into his coat and took out a huge chocolate bar which he dropped in the open violin case – it was all he had to donate. The bells were ringing changes at St. Mary's and we walked in the churchyard and listened.*

*Tomorrow we head on to Polbain. I am ready to settle down and get to work. We're ready to stop.*

It's a good six hours from Edinburgh to Coigach, maybe more. We drove north up the A9 through Perth and Pitlochry, crossed the great looming mountains at the Pass of Drumnadrochit, and descended through sparsely settled country to the bustling Highland capital of Inverness. From there we took a smaller road west, climbing over the spine of Britain at the desolate Dirrie Mor pass and down the far side to Loch Broom and the whitewashed village of Ullapool.

Out in the loch, a dozen huge dark ships swung at their anchors. Known as 'klondykers,' they are seagoing canneries from Bulgaria and Egypt and Germany, buying and processing the silvery fish mined by local boats from the rich waters off the Scottish coast. Closer in at the docks, a large ferry was loading cars and passengers for the daily trip down the loch to the open sea and Stornoway in the Outer Hebrides.

From Ullapool we followed the two-lane north for about ten miles to where, far from any sign of settlement, a lonely red telephone booth stands by the roadside. Just beyond, we turned off onto the single-track road toward Achiltibuie. Ahead lay a long narrow valley flanked by barren mountains that stood apart from each other like great Celtic standing stones. The single-track bobs and weaves its way along their flanks for a dozen miles, following the Garvie River as it runs down through pools, lochs and rushing falls to reach the sea. Nothing moved on the landscape except cloud shadows, our solitary car, and an occasional sheep scrambling to avoid us as we rounded curve after curve.

It was emptier than I had remembered, awesome as a moonscape and almost as devoid of life. For the first time, I felt doubts about what we were doing. Is this the country we'll be calling home for a year? What have we done?

All doubts fell away when we came at last to Polbain, where Wilf and Wendy welcomed us like long-lost family. We stayed the night at Sea View Cottage before venturing up the road to our new home at Castlehill.

# Autumn

## Castlehill

If you've ever seen Highland landscapes dotted with traditional cottages, you already know what Castlehill looks like: a small snug house with whitewashed walls, dark slate roof, a chimney at each end. Tucked deep into thick stone walls, two small windows flank an entry porch with a bright red painted door. Above, a pair of dormer windows peer out at the world. There is more to it than that, but that's what you'd see looking uphill from the road. Rowan trees with brilliant red berries are at the gate; in older times, folk believed they repelled witches. Lichen-covered drystone walls defend the property against encroaching purple heather.

Rising high behind the house is Castle Hill itself, a rocky knob on the side of a much larger hill – Meall an Fheadain, 'Hill of the Fairies' – that dominates the Coigach peninsula. Below the road, unused croft land runs down 200 yards to the edge of the sea. To the right of the house is an old stone steading, or barn, with an abandoned grinding wheel leaning against one corner.

We struggled with our luggage up the hill to the door. Coming in, I ran into the first clash between myself and the ways of the Highlands. Literally. The top of the doorway is about an inch lower than my scalp. This was the first of many wounds inflicted by local architecture. But the pain was quickly forgotten as I looked around. Although I'd never seen its like before, something about the old place felt familiar, snug, comforting.

Two doorways open off the entry hall. To the right is an empty, square room with a deep-set window facing Loch Broom. White painted tongue-and-groove wainscoting line the walls and ceiling. In front of the boarded-up fireplace stands an electric heater. I could imagine myself, the Great American Author, writing at my desk, looking up from my typewriter through the window to draw inspiration from the sea below. The daydream burst when I stepped in – and broke through the rotted flooring inside the doorway. Hmmm.

Across the entry hall is the lounge, an identical room but well furnished, with a drop-leaf table, two couches and a big deep chair next to the small tile fireplace. A big wooden wardrobe stands on one side, and there is a carpet spread on the floor. I stepped in gingerly; the floor felt nice and solid.

Castlehill was built in the late 19th century with two rooms downstairs and two bedrooms up. No electricity, no running water, no indoor toilet. Around 1940 an addition was put on the back, adding a "modern" kitchen, a third upstairs bedroom, and a full bathroom off the landing halfway up the stairs. This addition is simply a wood frame with corrugated iron outside, wainscoted walls and ceiling inside, and ambient (cold, damp) air in between.

The bathroom is long, narrow and unheated. The tub is long, narrow and looks like a horse trough. It is so long I could lie down flat in it without touching the ends. And so narrow I fear I might get stuck in it. And here I've discovered another cultural difference. In America, the hot water tap is always on the left, the cold on the right. In the Highlands, the hot water tap is on whichever side is closest to the water heater.

The two original bedrooms are small, with slanted ceilings front and back where the roof angles down, and one window apiece in tiny dormers letting light in from the south. Large knock-down wardrobes serve as closets, and there is a chest of drawers on the stairway landing between the rooms. Barb appropriated the room on the right for a studio, the other is now our bedroom. The back bedroom serves for occasional overnight guests.

But it is the kitchen of Castlehill that won our hearts. Stepping up one step from the back of the lounge, you come into a bright cozy room with a low ceiling. It is wainscoted and painted white like the other rooms, and filled with a lived-in jumble of appliances and furnishings. A full complement of dishes, flatware, pots and utensils cram the sideboard just inside the doorway. In the center is a table covered in oilcloth, with worn wooden chairs. Around the walls stand two tiny cube-like refrigerators stacked one on the other, a sink and cabinet, a washing machine with a separate wringer, and a very, very small stove and oven. The whole effect of the room was disorganized but homelike, a place where formality surrenders to convenience and comfort.

Outside the kitchen window, birds were picking at berries on another rowan tree. Barb ran water into a kettle and set it to heat while I rummaged in the sideboard for cups. In a few minutes, we were sitting down at the table for tea. After months of wandering, we were home.

# Settling In

Mildew. Black mildew. It covered the ceilings. It scattered in blotches across the walls. It lurked in dark corners, ever ready to race across neglected surfaces. Castlehill had been standing empty for some years, except for an occasional holiday rental. Every so often old Joan had been coming up to burn coal in the fireplace, trying to reduce the accumulating damp. But mildew is a virulent force in this coastal climate, and it took us a week of scrubbing with bleach to make the walls truly white again.

Joan had done her best to make the house livable, but there was much yet to do. I fixed up the office and patched the hole in the floor at the doorway. Barb rearranged the kitchen to suit her needs, aired all the cabinets, found places for the clothing and towels and linens and cooking gear she had brought from Minneapolis.

*September 3*

*Wilf and Wendy have just been fantastic – we never could have done everything without their help. Because it's been standing empty so long, the process of cleaning Castlehill and getting it set the way we want is a hard job – but is coming along nicely.*

*We have had gorgeous weather all week – until today when high winds have caused the electricity to go out – so we are using a gas light and little gas stove for making tea and have a fire going in the lounge. We have been busy every moment since we arrived. We've done our banking in Ullapool, bought an old red Austin Mini sedan in Dingwall, got groceries and tools in Inverness and bought wellies in Lochinver.*

Wellies – knee-high rubber boots – are more than the fashion here. They are essential for living in this world of seas and tides and bogs and sheep muck and driving rain. Intermittent rain if the weather's fair, constant if it's not. So rubber work boots are necessary not only for fishermen and crofters, but for gardeners, shoppers, school children, even – especially – for newcomers to the Highlands.

I soon learned that wellies don't guarantee dry feet. Wilf knew I was eager to get involved with local life, and phoned one day to tell me that his neighbor was gathering sheep on the croft below his house. I donned a white Irish sweater and shiny new wellies and hastened down the road to help.

Wilf introduced me to the crofter, a small, tough-looking, ruddy-faced man in bib overalls. He acknowledged me with a nod, his bright eyes squinting suspiciously, his thin lips clamped on a dead cigarette. We formed a line across the boggy croft and, shouting and waving, began chivvying the small group of sheep toward a pen. As I looked up at the distant mountains, cloud shadows skimming the purple heather, I was feeling quite pleased with myself – a kid from Chicago's crowded South Side, now working with sheep on a real Highland croft. Then I stepped into a hole.

The water was dark with peat and sheep muck, and deeper than my wellies. I felt the cold rush of it filling my boot as I sprawled on the wet ground. "Yipe!" I detected barely a hint of a smile on the crofter's face, but Wilf exploded in laughter when I picked myself up, trying to brush an accumulation of sheep turds from my once-white sweater.

That was my introduction to working with sheep, and to the crofter Wilf called Donnie-next-door.

# Game of the Name

You'd think that folks in a West Highland village would be known as MacThis or MacThat, but seldom do you hear MacAnything in Coigach. Not that folks here are reluctant to talk about each other – especially in the other's absence. At first, the names we heard in conversation were complete mysteries; names like The Post, The Captain, The Pest, The Plank, Dodo, The Pudding, Ann Ha'penny, even Simon Schoolbus. But there is a certain logic to this, as there is to all West Highland ways.

Consider that, of the 200 people scattered in small settlements around the Coigach peninsula, close to half seem to be Macleods or Mackenzies. And countless Ians, Murdos and Alasdairs, Kennys and Donnies, Anns and Mairis and Joans are scattered across the landscape. A conversational reference to Murdo Macleod or Ian Mackenzie is of little use – it could mean any one of half a dozen people. To solve the problem, identifying nicknames evolved.

There are vocational names, much like the Bakers, Butchers, Farmers and Smiths you've seen clustered in your phone directory – but not yet frozen in place: Kenny School the schoolmaster, Donnie Post the postman, and the aforementioned Simon Schoolbus who drives the children to school. But also descriptive names such as Big Leslie (a large woman) and Wee Leslie (a small man). There are humorous names like Kenny Pest the teenager, Ann Ha'penny the tightfisted shopkeeper, and – for a man who seems bent on telling everyone else what to do – the Manager. Some people bear names of uncertain origin: Roll, Hand, West,  names invented a generation past, and handed down to everyone in the family. A few are identified by the name of the place they live, such as Murdo and Jimmy Badenscallie – or where they're from, like Anne Irish.

To confuse matters further, sometimes the names can change. For example, when we first came to Coigach our mail was delivered by Donnie Post. When Donnie Post retired, he became Donnie Roll, and his replacement, Ali West, became Ali Post.

These are names of convenience, usually used in conversation to identify third parties not present. But they are seldom used when you speak to the person himself. Thus the rotund and benign young man everyone knows as 'The Pudding' is commonly addressed as Alan. And you'd always use his proper name to greet the gentle young man widely known as 'The Plank' – "so thick," folks say, "you would need a hammer to pound an idea into him." Even here there are exceptions – everyone calls William Sinclair 'Boysie,' a name first used by his mother. 'Stookie', derived from the Gaelic for someone a bit slow, is one of the few fond pejoratives used even by the man himself.

As feminism has not yet penetrated the West, a woman is sometimes identified by her husband's name. Ali Beag – in Gaelic, Little Ali – is a Macleod whose father was called Ali Mor, or Big Ali. His wife is known as 'Ann Ali Beag', and their family is called 'The Ali Beags.' I once heard a married woman identified by her father's name, as 'Mairi Murdo William.' And, to her chagrin, Barb is occasionally called 'Mrs. Jack.'

Adding to the confusion, some people have several nicknames. The crofter Wilf calls Donnie-next-door is more commonly known as Donnie Darling (his mother had called him so) but sometimes called Curly or Coyote for no apparent reason. Wee Les is occasionally called The Poet. In fact, the nickname can be almost any convenient word invented on the spot, so long as it clearly identifies the person being discussed.

To distinguish me from another Jack in the community, someone might refer to me as Jack Polbain (our village), Jack Castlehill (our cottage), American Jack, Jack Barbara (yes, it could happen), or Bugsy (from a current film 'Bugsy Malone'). For all I know, there may be other nicknames I haven't heard. And might not want to hear.

So next time you run into one of those Scots-Americans who tend to be a bit pompous about his clan MacThis or MacThat, you can have fun imagining what he might be called in a real Highland village where everyone else shared the name!

# Crofts, Crofters and the Laird

The laird of Badentarbat Estate owns all the land that forms Coigach peninsula, the land on which the hamlets of Polbain, Altandhu, Reiff and Achnahaird stand, the land on which Castlehill sits. It all belongs to the laird. Yet it is also a birthright belonging to many of the people who live here. This is due to history and a peculiarity of Scottish law.

After Bonnie Prince Charlie was defeated at Culloden in 1745, the Highland clans were broken and their lands went into private ownership. Wealthy individuals acquired immense estates – many thousands of acres – populated by impoverished tenants renting crofts.

Crofts are bits of arable land eked out from hill and mountain, small fields for raising a few subsistence crops, or keeping a cow or some chickens. The land is hard and poor, and croft boundaries are usually defined by drystone dikes – unmortared walls built by careful fitting of rocks delved from the soil itself. Few can support a family on what a croft alone will yield, so most croft tenants turn to the sea or the hills for other work to keep themselves alive.

By the early 1800s, the landowners, or lairds, discovered that sheep had become worth more to them than rents from their tenants. In what became notorious as the Highland Clearances, tens of thousands of crofters were evicted to make way for sheep. Many left Scotland forever, emigrating to North America, far Australia or New Zealand. Those who remained struggled fiercely against law and laird to retain their historic place on the land. And the people of Coigach were among the most tenacious – and imaginative.

In 1853, a sheriff and some policemen set out from Ullapool to serve the laird's eviction notices on a group of crofters in Achiltibuie, Badenscallie and Culnacraig. No road to Coigach existed at the time, so the authorities rowed down Loch Broom in a longboat. Word of their mission raced overland ahead of them, and the community determined to resist. To put the sheriff and his crew off their guard, local men donned women's clothing and gathered on the beach. When the would-be evicters tried to land their boat, the crofters mobbed them. Some of the policemen were literally stunned by the ferocity of the Coigach "women." They drove off the police, burned the eviction papers at the water's edge, and stripped the sheriff of his trousers, sending him naked back to Ullapool.

In 1886, the struggles of crofters throughout the Highlands were rewarded with the passage of the Crofting Act, guaranteeing the right of tenants to hold, sell, or pass on to their heirs the crofts on which they were living. They could no longer be evicted, or forced out by unreasonable rents. The lairds still owned the land, but crofters owned the use of it, including rights to common grazing on the estates.

Given that history, the relationship between crofter and laird in the Highlands has often been less than friendly. But on Badentarbat Estate, it is different. The laird is well liked, even loved – tall and distinguished, an accomplished fly fisher, a painter trained at the Slade School of Fine Arts, an adventurer credited for pioneering a climbing route in Jordan. Impeccably dressed in tweed suits and a smart fore-and-aft cap reminiscent of Sherlock Holmes, Mrs. Longstaff is a remarkable woman.

Charmian Longstaff and her husband Tom had bought the estate after World War II. Born in 1875, Tom was a true Victorian, born to wealth and privilege. Oxford-educated, he was trained in medicine but never had need for a practice. Instead, the young doctor applied his skills as a passport to global adventure. He was chief medical officer and naturalist on many early British expeditions to the Alps, the Himalayas and the Arctic, including the 1922 Everest Expedition. Later, he became president of the Royal Geographical Society and the Alpine Club.

During World War I, Tom served as an officer on the frontier of Empire, leading native Gilgit Scouts in the Hindu Kush where the game of polo originated. Whenever his mounted troops entered a remote Himalayan village, tradition demanded that they test their skills against the local riders. In his classic mountaineering autobiography This My Voyage, Longstaff describes the distinctive wound that ended his wartime service: "I was invalided home in October 1917, as a result of a direct hit on the temple by a rising polo ball."

One war later, Tom met Charmian in London during the Blitz – a time she later recalled as being the most exciting of her life. "You never knew when a bomb might come down and kill you," she told us, "but I never felt more alive." They married not long after, and retired to Scotland. When Tom died in 1964, Charmian stayed on as laird of the estate. She lives in Badentarbat Lodge, a large house crammed with exotic artifacts from Tom's expeditions. It is here that all tenants on the estate come, once a year, to pay their annual rent.

Rent Day is an Occasion. Scrubbed and buffed and dressed in their Sunday best, crofters come to the Lodge one by one throughout the afternoon. Mrs. Longstaff pours a generous dram for each arrival. For a few minutes, they discuss conditions on the croft and in the community, about which she is well informed and deeply interested.

In Britain, the way one pronounces words can define the gulf between social classes. The laird speaks in the plummy accent of privilege, the crofter in the measured tones of the rural Highlands. Yet their shared love of the land is a bridge linking them together, and their conversation is friendly and down-to-earth. Warmed by the laird's welcome – and no little bit of whisky – the crofter departs the Lodge in jolly mood and ready to join his neighbors for a few more drams at the Fuaran.

I can't imagine how Charmian Longstaff survives the parade of visitors on Rent Day, for I can attest that the gracious laird would never let a visitor drink alone.

## September 4

*I spent the morning cleaning and ironing. The iron works fine, thank goodness. The washing machine on the other hand is broken and we have to do our washing by hand and crank it through the wringer. Hopefully we can get it at least partially operable again.*

*We took a run into Ullapool this afternoon to do some banking and shopping. It takes 45 minutes just to get to the small shops there, and 2 ½ hours to get to the nearest real stores in Inverness, so we have to buy in bulk and plan carefully. The drive is a pleasure, though – the streams and mountains dramatic in the changing light. It is so unbelievably beautiful here.*

*Jack has been out sea fishing twice already and we've had meals of crab, mackerel (delicious when fresh from the sea), and whiting so far. The last time he was out they had porpoises playing around the boat for about 15 minutes – diving under it and slapping it with their tails. We saw a seal the other day too.*

*High winds and the first rain since we arrived in Britain caused a power outage that lasted from 5:00 – 10:00 p.m. We had a sandwich supper and borrowed a gas lantern and camping stove from Bells. The coal fire is going in the lounge, but doesn't seem to provide much heat. Wilf says that it will improve once the heat works into the stone walls. I hope so – or the winter may be cold.*

*We've also done quite a bit of visiting with Murdo and Joan Macleod, our landlords.*

# Murdo and Joan

To distinguish him from all the other Murdo Macleods in Coigach, the old man who owns Castlehill is widely known as Dodo. But because he is the first Murdo we have known, and has become such a part of our lives, to us 'Murdo' always means our Murdo and none other.

The house where Murdo and his sister Joan live stands well back from the road. An isolated place for a now isolated life. You can't get within earshot without triggering an explosion of barking and snarling from inside, the sound of a cane thumping ribs, and Joan's voice crying "Cap! No! Enough! Cap!" Cap is Murdo's dog. Once a swift-running master of the hills whose glaring eye put fear in the hearts of sheep, the old dog is now confined to crouching through the days by the side of his house-bound master. One wary eye is always open, one ear listening for a chance to do his only remaining duty and pleasure: intimidation.

Inside, the house bears signs of a long and losing struggle against darkness, damp and age. There are always a few lumps of coal smoldering in the cramped tile fireplace. Close by, trying to absorb its feeble warmth, Murdo sits through the days, a once-vigorous man weakened by stroke, now almost motionless in the traditional pride of place: the bodach's chair – the old man's chair by the fireside. Accentuated by his strong jaw, Murdo's mouth has a sucked-in look without his store-bought teeth. The upper plate must not fit well, for he keeps it in the pocket of his woolen cardigan, only fishing it out and popping it into his mouth at meal times. I always worry about lint in the pocket.

Joan puts all her energy into taking care of her brother, and anyone else who steps across the threshold. She is small, grey and wizened. Arthritis has turned her hands into gnarly claws, and her wispy hair struggles to escape the old-fashioned hairpins she wears. Yet her eyes are bright, and somewhere beneath her years is a pretty young girl with a thirst for life and a generous heart. No Mayfair hostess could make us feel more welcome. She scuttles around the house, making tea and setting out little plates of buttered pancakes, cookies, or candy bars.

Murdo and Joan were born on Tanera Mor, the island about a mile offshore from Polbain, in a time when Gaelic was the everyday tongue and every man in Coigach won his living from the hills and the sea. Tanera had once been the center of a thriving herring fishery in Loch Broom: a snug anchorage for the 19th century sailing ships that carried salt herring from the island's processing factory to the cities of Scotland and England and the Continent. The long, curved stone pier where the herring barrels were taken on board, depicted in a print by William Daniell published in 1820, is still used by the small motor boats that tend the salmon cages in Tanera's anchorage.

The settlement on Tanera peaked in the mid-1800's, and was already long in decline by WWI. Yet even in Murdo's youth the island could support three or four fishing boats, crewed by farmer-fishermen. These were still sailing boats, for the first internal combustion engines only reached the Northwest Highlands after the Great War. The boats of Tanera Mor were single masted craft, with a crew of four men to ply the oars and handle the gaff-rigged sails. In the winter, they set lobster traps among the islands; in summer, they trailed long lines to catch haddock and herring and cod. Some of the fish they could sell to the hotel in Achiltibuie for cash; most they kept for feeding their families.

By 1930, the population of Tanera had dropped to the point where only one fishing boat could be crewed. And when one of the crew decided to move to the mainland, the other families had to leave too – for the island economy was such that no family could survive without the fishing, and it needed four to put out a boat. That's why Murdo and Joan wound up on the mainland in Polbain.

Even in her seventies, Joan has an irrepressible girlish charm about her. The aging spinster seems to have adopted us as the children she never had, and lavishes attention on us we seldom deserve. An endless procession of teas, cakes, her special clootie dumplings and other treats come from Joan's tiny kitchen to welcome us, and the only time we have disagreements is when she tries to lower the modest rent we pay for Castlehill.

Before WWII, the roads between Coigach and the great cities of Scotland were difficult at best. Along the wild west coast, the shopping needs of isolated communities like Coigach were served weekly by puffers – small flat-bottomed cargo steamers capable of going in to shallow anchorages, or even being beached at high tide, for the convenience of coastal customers. Puffers were floating super-stores. Almost anything, from farm machinery, tires and boat engine parts to clothing, shoes and bicycles could be ordered for delivery on the next boat. Murdo says that when the puffer was still coming in to Badentarbat every week, he was in charge of the pier. He also had the mail concession for Tanera and had to make the run twice a week no matter what the weather.

When the puffer came in with its merchandise, news of the outside world came with it. I've been told that young Joan was always the first to race up the puffer's gangplank to get the latest word, and the first to come down and report it. Even years later, her instinct for gossip is uncanny – she always seems to know the news before it happens.

Jim Muir hinted to us that Joan had "the powers," as had her mother before her. After a near-miss attack from Joan's border collie, Sandy Boots said he'd be willing to shoot the dog except that Joan might fashion a wee dollie of him and stick pins in it. These tales were told in jest. Sort of.

Like so many young women in the Highlands, where opportunities have always been limited, Joan emigrated to the cities. She worked in London for a while, and in Paisley, and loved the city life. But eventually she came back to Coigach when her mother was dying, and then stayed on to take care of Murdo. Joan is as small as Murdo is large, and helping the big man move about the house must be difficult. But she is a strong woman in every way, and maybe "the powers" help.

## September 6

*Joan came up this morning to bring some prawns she had gotten for us from the fish man yesterday. She also wanted to return some of the rent we had given them – said that £15 per week was too much and that they had decided to make it £12 instead. We then had a big argument as to how much we were going to pay – and we won, so it's left at £15 a week, which is still ridiculously low for a fully furnished three bedroom house. Honestly – I think if we let them keep on, pretty soon they'd be paying us. It's ridiculous!*

*This afternoon we climbed over the fence behind the house and scrambled to the top of Castle Hill. The view is beautiful from up there – a panorama from Suilven and Stac Pollaidh all the way around to An Teallach and An-t-Sail in the Dundonnels across Loch Broom. There was a terrific wind blowing and the clouds were racing across the sky – constantly changing the landscape. The heather is in bloom and I'm filling the house with bunches of it. So things here are wonderful and we're quite happy.*

*September 8*

*Took the day off and went for a walk up the peat road. The hills were thick with heather and although the sky was cloudy the view of the mountains and islands was clear. I met our next door neighbor, Ian Macdonald, as he was coming out to walk his dog. He took me in to meet his wife, Joy, and I stayed for tea. They asked us to dinner on Wednesday.*

*Jack was fishing this afternoon and came home with a load of coal fish which we fried up for supper. They're my favorite so far – sweet and delicious. Our days are full and pleasantly tiring, and each night we sit by the fire and talk. I haven't slept so well in years.*

# Old Boys

The house next door where Joy lives is called Mullagrach, so named because her husband Ian has acquired the island of Mullagrach which is just west of Isle Ristol and the mouth of Old Dorney harbor. Ian has no more use for an island than you or I, but ownership gives him a connection to the Highlands which – to a staunch member of the Scottish National Party – seems significant.

Ian and his wife Joy are incomers, retired to Polbain from Edinburgh where he had been a solicitor. More generous neighbors you couldn't want, and we spend many an evening with them and their dearest friends Arthur and Evelyn. Arthur is retired also, having been chief anaesthesiologist at Raigmore Hospital in Inverness.

The two men went to school together as boys growing up in Edinburgh, then went their separate ways – Ian to India as a circuit judge, Arthur to medical school and the British army in World War II. Both have long and harrowing stories of their adventures – in dusty villages during the Raj, in desperate combat at Dunkirk – which they love to spin out over a good dram or two after a good dinner. But sooner or later the conversation turns to weightier matters, and you can sense, in the talk between the two aging men, more than a hint of schoolyard taunting.

Ian, slow talking, vague, deliberate as only pipe smokers can be, has a sly way of piercing Arthur's inflated rhetoric. And Arthur, neat, quick and jovial, jabs and slices at Ian's seriousness. Both men are well read and well armed to do battle over history, politics, philosophy, literature. The subject doesn't matter, so long as they can take opposite sides and argue the night away. If the debate lags for even a moment, Arthur can be counted on to take a poke at the Scottish National Party, which Ian will promptly defend, and they're off to war again.

Being committed to neither side in these verbal conflicts, and somewhat naive as well, I try to seek and expound on common ground – which neither man really wants to occupy. So the war of words between the two Old Boys is never resolved. At the end of the evening each declares victory and marches off to his own mental fortress, to emerge next time ready for another battle.

Barb, Joy and Evelyn often escape to the kitchen after dinner, where they make tea and prepare treats and can laugh at their husbands' nonsense.

## September 10th

*Today we had the first really bad weather since we came here. It's raining and blowing and worse is predicted. So we've had a cheery fire going all afternoon and I've spent the day writing letters etc. and enjoying doing nothing.*

*Yesterday I finished cleaning my studio area – the last room in the house to be finished. It all looks so nice and really feels like home to me now. In the afternoon we walked over the hills to Loch na Beiste so that Jack could do some fly fishing. The day was cool and windy, but sunny, so we had a lovely walk – and he caught a nice brown trout which we grilled along with some venison chops for supper.*

*We met a chap who was driving along the road and stopped to talk to us. He had his sheepdog lying in his lap, another small dog in the passenger seat, and a sheep sitting quietly in the back seat! He told Jack where all the good fishing spots were and chatted for quite a while.*

*That evening we went to see Joan and Murdo for a visit, and asked them about the fellow we'd met. They said that everyone here calls him "The Manager" because he tries to manage everyone's business. Murdo was in excellent humor and was more animated than I've ever seen him. I hope he decides to go to Dingwall on Thursday for the sheep market. Joan fed us tea and goodies and insisted that we take her torch again to go home. The moon was bright enough to see just fine – but she will not let us leave without a flashlight!*

# Dingwall Market

Far over the crest of the mountains, down toward the east coast, is the town where Coigach's crofters bring their ewe and wether lambs every autumn. Market Day in Dingwall is an annual event. Sheep men from all over the region come together to sell the product of their spring and summer labors, and afterward gather at pubs with old acquaintances to celebrate their gains or mourn their losses.

It takes all week to prepare for Market Day: gathering sheep in from the hill to Coigach's scattered fanks, separating castrated wether lambs and ewe lambs from their mothers, choosing which to keep and which to sell, loading them into lorries for the long haul over the Dirrie Mor pass. Then the crofters dress in their finest, take their best rams-horn handled crooks from the wall, and – still wearing wellies, of course – drive off for the day to Dingwall.

*September 12*

*Murdo did finally decide to come, I was glad to see. He has a lot of old friends there that he seldom sees. We left early and did some shopping (Dingwall has a prize-winning haggis maker) and then met Wilf, Donnie and Alasdair West at the sale barn pens. Jack helped with the sorting while Murdo and I went inside to watch the bidding. What an assortment of characters – hopeful sellers and stone-faced buyers, polished gentry and calloused crofters – all with tweed jackets though! One by one, small groups of lambs were herded into the ring. I couldn't understand what the auctioneer was saying and the bidding for each lot was done with no visable sign that I could detect. Blackface lambs seemed to bring better prices then Cheviots – but for the most part people around Coigach raise Cheviots. The prices weren't as good as they have been for the last few years.*

*We left the market about 1:00 to do some shopping in Inverness – picked up our new bottled gas heater and groceries in quantity. On the way back we stopped for dinner and a pint at Altguish. There is a big dam on the river there with the hotel right below it. They have a cozy pub with dark beams and a warm fire – and good pub food.*

# Salt Herring

The road home from Dingwall Sale to Coigach is long and dark and fraught with more than a few tempting pubs. There were no signs of life in Polbain when I walked through the next morning, until I got to the Nissen hut where Jim Muir is often found tending his fishing gear. Compact and lithe, a man of middle years with a quick smile and leathery good looks, Jim loves to tell Coigach stories. He was sitting on a wooden crate and repairing the netting on a lobster creel, but didn't hesitate to put his work aside.

"Oh, the day after the lamb sale is always quiet," he nodded, "the lads have to have their fun." A bit of mischief flashed in his eyes. "Did you hear about the time Dodo and Angus – who had Castlehill then – managed to drink all night from a tinker's purse on the way home from Dingwall sale?" He turned up another crate and bade me sit a while.

The story that followed took place during World War II, when German submarines were active around the Hebrides. Murdo and Angus were out fishing, and retrieved a sealed and brass-bound wooden chest they found bobbing along on the incoming tide. Packed inside were bundles of newly printed Nationalist Chinese currency. Thinking at first that they had found their fortune, they were soon disappointed by the Ullapool banker; the money was virtually worthless outside of Chiang Kai-Shek's dwindling Kuomintang territory. But they tucked a few stacks of bills in their pockets and brought them to Dingwall sheep sale, thinking they might have some fun, at least.

On the way home that night, they stopped – as we had done – for some refreshment at the pub in Altguish. And there they met a tinker, who wanted to sell them an old horse. The light in the pub was weak as the drink was strong. So when the Coigach men flashed their bundles of crisp blue currency, the tinker became inspired. He bought round after round with intent to divest these slow-talking crofters of their obvious wealth. Without close examination of money or horse, a deal was struck near closing time, and the horse trader wandered happily off to bed.

Jim told me the boys returned laughing to Coigach in the night, with their sheep sale proceeds intact. And the tinker awoke in the morning with a pocketful of Chinese money, a monumental bar bill, and his sorry-looking steed still waiting outside.

As a newcomer I expect to have my leg pulled once in a while, and I guess I looked a bit skeptical. Jim grinned, stood up and went to dig around in his cluttered hut. He came out and handed me two crisp blue bills that looked a bit like the £5 notes issued by the Royal Bank of Scotland. But they were Chinese. And they had consecutive serial numbers.

Jim Muir is something of a keeper of traditional ways. He and his wife Aileen have a craft shop in a little white cottage attached to their house in Polbain, where tourists can find hand-knit woolens and artwork and a welcoming cup of tea. Jim fishes for salmon from an old wooden Orkney boat whose neat, brightly painted lines grace Old Dornie harbor.

"Have you had salt herring yet?" His eyes were dancing.

"No, but I've read about it."

He reached into a barrel beside the hut and pulled out a couple of dessicated fish, their sides sparkling with salt crystals. "This is the real traditional Coigach mainstay – about all that people had to keep them through the winters in times past." He carefully wrapped the fish in paper and told me how to prepare salt herring. "Now, be sure to soak these well. And serve them with boiled tatties and a little butter. You won't need to salt anything."

I brought Jim's gift back to Castlehill, and Barb prepared the fish for supper that night. The herring were tasty enough, but Jim was right – they were so salty that the unseasoned potatoes were needed for relief.

That night, I relived a past experience in a nightmare. It was hot and dry, and I was crossing the sands of the African Sahel, my tongue swollen and throat parched, desperate to reach a distant oasis for a drop of cool water. I sat up suddenly in the dark. It was cold and damp, but my throat really was parched, my tongue was swollen. I scrambled down to the bathroom and ran the tap for a long time before my thirst was slaked.

Next time I saw Jim Muir I told him about my nightmare. "Oh," he laughed, "I forgot to tell you – we always eat salt herring at midday, so we have time to drink enough water before bed time."

## September 13

*Yesterday went with W&W to hear the Ullapool Junior Pipe Band, which includes several youngsters from Coigach. Each year they come up to perform in the schoolyard here. Their teacher was Regimental Pipe Major for the Seaforth Highlanders, and he ran off one solo on his bagpipe that was really beautiful. We sat on a stone wall watching as they marched back and forth with the pipes skirling and the mountains, islands and the sea in the background.*

*The band is very good for kids that age (11-15 yrs.) and they have even been invited to play for the Queen. It was delightful to hear the pipes in the open air like that!*

## September 16th

*I finally got some sketching in – did a drawing of the shed in back where we keep our coal, and the rowan tree outside the kitchen window. I've gotten quite fond of that view. Also have been able to do some guitar practicing and I've enjoyed that.*

*This morning Jack finally went down to Wilf's to pick up the lumber and tools for making his desk. Wilf was cleaning Frieda's feet and spraying her for foot rot – a disease where the hoof rots away if it's not treated. Nasty. Anyway the desk came out well and is now set up in the office. Soon he will have to begin work.*

*The pace of life here is impossible for you to imagine; it's like going back to the 18th century. No one hurries, yet time passes quickly. We have no TV, nor do we miss it. Our best* entertainment is to walk down the road to visit Wilf or Murdo, or stroll down to the harbor at Old Dornie, enjoying the play of light and shadow on the sea and islands and mountains across the loch. The weather changes constantly and rapidly, and almost every day brings sun and rain, warmth and wind and an evening chill to make the fire welcome.

## September 18th

Jack is in the kitchen boiling a pig's head. I am avoiding the whole scene. We bought half a pig from Simon Macleod the butcher in Lochinver – all cut up and boxed for only 65p/lb. When we unpacked it, though, we found a neatly split half a pig's head! I'm not used to looking my groceries in the eye and was all for throwing it away, but Jack asked around Polbain and found a recipe for what they call 'brawn' which is the same as head cheese in America. If he wants it, he'll have to make it.

The vet came yesterday from east of Dingwall and made house calls, taking care of all the veterinary needs in this area. Wilf's Frieda got her feet trimmed and got an antibiotic injection, and Murdo's dogs got their nails trimmed and several local cats were remodeled.

## September 19th

The pig's head production was successful! After the head had simmered with bay leaves, parsley, garlic and peppercorns for two hours or so Jack let it cool and removed it from the pot. The broth was boiled down to about 1½ pints. He cleaned the meat off the skull, cut it up and put it into a bread pan. The reduced stock was poured over that and another bread pan put on top and weighted with soup cans to press the loaf as it jelled. I sliced some for a sandwich this afternoon – it was delicious!

The sunset tonight was incredible. It's impossible to describe the beauty of the shifting light and shadow – the scene changes – a mountain top picked out and outlined in gold one minute will become a misty blue the next – ridges and valleys will be clear and *then just disappear again. The sky was a painter's dream – colors from velvety blue & gray to gold, pink and purple – clouds edged in pink or gold – the sea like liquid shining silver. Tanera looked like it was made of crushed velvet. A more beautiful evening I can't remember.*

# Highland Cuisine

In this nation of scattered villages, shopkeepers serving remote communities have to stock merchandise with a long shelf life, to make up for the slow turnover of their inventories. This is certainly the case in Coigach, where the small shops – one each in Achiltibuie and Polbain – stock everything from fishing tackle, shoelaces, candles, gloves, batteries, sewing needles and dog biscuits, to basic groceries – the last well laced with the chemical cocktails we call preservatives. If you're looking to find fresh food, you'll do better looking elsewhere. So you might well ask, "what is your food like?"

The surprising answer is, very good, thank you. But it doesn't come easy.

The best of our provender comes from the sea. Days spent with Wilf on his little *Annabelle* bring home boxes of fresh mackerel, codling, saith and coal fish. Other days helping Peter Drake on *Sea Swallow* yield prawns, the occasional lobster, and buckets of the little clawless spiny lobsters whose tails have no market value but make wonderful additions to casseroles. Neighbors and friends bring us big brown crabs (cancer pagurus, the aptly named 'edible crab') caught in traps along the shore and among the islands. And fresh wild salmon, if an otter has taken a chunk from it that makes it unfit for market. We've also enjoyed poached salmon that was grilled – I won't explain that, but leave it to your imagination.

It has taken some learning. Wilf gave me lessons in filleting fish, although so far my fillets come out more like fishburger. Barb has drawn from seafood recipes in Delia Smith's Cookery Course, which we found at the excellent little bookshop in Inverkirkaig. The hardest part, really, is cooking live crabs and lobsters. 'They' say that putting these crustaceans in cold water and slowly bringing up the heat will put them to sleep without a struggle. 'They' lie. It takes a while to get used to fending off your dinner with a wooden spoon as it struggles to climb out of the pot.

*We spent this morning cleaning crabs – cracking the shells & removing the meat. The soft material inside the rim of the shell – what Downeasters call the 'tomally' – Jack made into a delicious pate (crab, vinegar, salt, pepper & breadcrumbs).*

Di Wilding, a strikingly pretty young lass from Cornwall whose husband Lance works at the fishing, has shared some of the rabbits she snares. Donnie Darling brought over a delicious sheep liver after I helped him recover some ewes from the islands. Margaret West has given us tasty guinea fowl eggs – diminutive eggs with pointed ends and the toughest shells you've ever tried to crack. I can't recall who brought us fresh sea gull eggs from nests on the islands – they were bigger than chicken eggs and had a strong eggy flavor, which made them wonderful for baking.

Others – who shall remain nameless – have donated venison 'found' on the hill after dark. One such 'found' deer was stashed in the back of the poacher's Land Rover and concealed with a tarp. Pleased with his illicit success, the man stopped in the Fuaran for a celebratory pint. When he came back out to his car, the deer was propped bolt upright in the driver's seat, its forefeet neatly poised on the steering wheel.

Our major grocery shopping is done on bi-weekly outings to the supermarket in Inverness, which has everything a Scot could want – but lacks a few items we Americans need. Like popcorn, available only at a tiny health food store tucked into an old back lane. And Crisco and cranberries and pumpkin pie filling and chocolate chips for cookies – items occasionally smuggled across the Atlantic by visiting friends.

Exploring the grocery shelves, Barb found ample evidence of the old saying that Americans and Brits "are separated by a common language."

*In the sugar display they had "caster," "granulated," "soft brown," "icing" and "demerara." These weren't too hard to figure out except that I don't know what "caster" sugar is. There was no such thing as molasses or corn syrup so I got "treacle" and "golden syrup" instead, figuring they might be close.*

*I wanted to get some zucchini and eggplant in Inverness for making ratatouille – the clerk just looked at me with this blank expression and said they didn't have any such things. I asked Wendy about it later and she explained that zucchini are called "marrows" here – and eggplants are "aubergines."*

Bread was a problem, at first – the packaged bread here is less than appetizing. Think Wonder Bread, but without all the texture and flavor. Home baking was an attractive option – Barb actually enjoys it – but her first attempts were frustrated by the unfamiliar labels and ingredients.

*I stood in the shop's baking section for a long time staring at the truly bewildering displays of simple things like sugar and flour. At home I used all-purpose flour for all my baking. Simple. Here I had to make a choice between 'plain,' 'strong,' 'self-rising,' 'superfine' or a number of other flours designated by percentages. 'Plain' seemed as close to all-purpose as I could come so I chose that.*

*I took out my favorite bread recipe and made a couple loaves. It looked fine – but when I tried to slice it, it was more like trying to cut into one of those plaster display models. Yuck! So the next day I tried a shorter baking time – producing what turned into a sodden lump. Despair!*

*Went next door to Joy's this afternoon and learned what I've been doing wrong. My biggest problem was the flour – "plain" flour is only used for cakes or puddings. "Strong" flour is what you need for bread, and Joy's turned out perfectly – so I'll have to make all our bread from now on. She has a stove called an Aga which runs on oil and keeps warm all day – heats the kitchen and the hot water and works on the order of an old-fashioned wood stove. Cozy.*

Cockburn's in Dingwall is our source for some of the best haggis in Scotland. Haggis? Yes, haggis – that mysterious, legendary Scottish dish cooked inside the stomach of a sheep. You may curl a lip with revulsion. But consider this: you have probably enjoyed good 'old fashioned' sausages packed in pigs' intestines – which are considerably farther downstream in the digestive tract!

Jimmy, a musician friend from over the mountains in Portmahomack, informs me that haggis are wild hill creatures, adapted to their slanting world by growing legs longer on the right side than the left. They graze counter-clockwise around and around their mountain, kept level by their long legs bracing on the down side. Wily Highland hunters stalk the haggis, armed with a staghorn whistle. When they blow a sharp note on it, the startled beasts turn around and – shorter legs now downhill – tumble to their doom.

I have since learned that haggis is sheep liver, lungs, and heart, chopped fine and mixed with pinhead oatmeal, salt and pepper, suet, onions, herbs and spices, packed and cooked inside a natural casing (the sheep's stomach). In other words, it is simply a form of sausage. And made well, it is delicious. If the stomach bit bothers you, fear not – most haggis today is cooked in large commercial sausage casings just like your favorite salami. The haggis we buy at Cockburn's is packaged thus. We slice it into hockey-puck size servings and keep it in the freezer, to be brought out every Wednesday night, toasted under the grill, and served with diced turnips, mashed potatoes and a dram of whisky.

*I finally succeeded in making nice, crusty bread today. I'd almost forgotten how much better home-baked bread is! It's nice to have time to do that again. Our new freezer now has half a venison, half a pig, loads of fish of different kinds, haggis and bread. We're pretty well set for the winter.*

## The Fuaran

If you're looking for a little entertainment, the latest local news, some friendly conversation, or simply an escape from the confines of home, you can almost always find it in a pub. In Coigach, the largest and most popular is the Fuaran, just above the road at Altandhu. The entrance is flanked by two bedraggled palm trees which look as natural as hula skirts in the Arctic. A few windows in the plain public bar look out on a small car park and beyond to Isle Ristol and Loch Broom. Leaning on the bar inside, you can see any familiar car pulling into the car park – a convenience that allows you time to have a dram set up for its driver when he pushes through the door. The room is spare, furnished with a couple of tables with chairs, a darts board in a corner, and a tile floor convenient for mopping up traces of sheep shit tracked in on patrons' wellies .

If you come into the Fuaran to pour out your troubles and seek comfort, you'll be disappointed. Andy, the publican, always has more troubles than you, and he's glad of the opportunity to bend your ear about them. To hear him talk, the government, the weather and the VAT are all conspiring to drive him out of business, and it's only as a favor to you that he keeps the Fuaran open. An earnest, well meaning but cheerless sort, Andy can lay on a blanket of depression that only lifts when pretty Margaret the barmaid relieves him, and brightens the room with her smile.

At the back, and a step or two up, is the lounge bar, discreetly set apart from the public bar by tartan curtains and floored with industrial carpeting. The long windowless room has subdued lighting and is decorated in Flotsam Chic – a life ring, glass fishing floats, bits of brass and scraps of net – just in case anyone fails to notice the Fuaran's proximity to the sea. Here there are padded banquettes and stools, small tables, and in pride of place, an undersized, coin-operated pool table. There is a short menu of pub food, nicely prepared in a kitchen out back and served by the publican's wife Siona.

Outside of the tourist season, the Fuaran is generally pleasant, uncrowded except on weekends, and decidedly local. The first week night I stopped in, Ali Beag and Simon Schoolbus were back in the lounge bar, working out some Gaelic music on button accordion and fiddle. I was the sole audience, and I think Simon would have preferred none at all, but the tunes were lovely in a home-made sort of way, and I went home quite happy to have heard them.

On Friday evenings and Saturdays in winter, and almost any time in summer, the Fuaran is busy, blue with smoke and thrumming with conversation. Access to the jammed downstairs bar can be difficult, and sometimes thirsty patrons nip up to a pass-through bar in the lounge where they can outflank the crowd below and catch Andy's attention. But most days, most of the year, it serves as a cozy and convenient social hub where you can pick up all the latest news of Coigach – the fishing, the sheep, the weather – and debate all the issues of the great world.

# Peter Drake

I feared the Mini's lower radiator hose had sprung a leak on the way home from Ullapool. The little red car stood, bonnet raised and steaming, outside the tiny garage below Castlehill. On closer inspection, however, the problem was more serious. I crawled out from beneath and was standing disconsolate, pondering a major breakdown with nothing but a hammer and screwdriver, when my next door neighbor came down.

"Problem?" A young man, tall, slender, blond.

"Yeah. The radiator is cracked, right where the lower hose attaches."

"Mmm."

"I suppose I'll have to have it towed in to Ullapool."

"Oh, that shouldn't be necessary. I think Hector might fix it for you." He stuck out a hand: "I'm Peter Drake."

The handshake and prompt introduction was unusual in Coigach, and so is Peter Drake, as I would later learn. He was on his way to Ullapool and couldn't stop to help, but he loaned me tools from his own garage and told me how to find Hector the Mechanic, who had the farm at Achnahaird and fixed whatever ailed the cars of Coigach.

I struggled and cursed for an hour to pry the tiny radiator out of the car, then tucked it under my arm and set out on foot for Achnahaird. By the time I got there, I was no longer sure which place was Hector the Mechanic's. He had posted no convenient sign or billboard advertising his services. After all, everyone in Coigach knows who and where he is – everyone but me. Naturally, there was no one around. So I placed the car part by the door of my best guess, with a note explaining the problem and my Castlehill address, and walked back to Polbain in the evening light.

Next morning there came a knock at the door. When I opened it, a perky young woman stood there with my radiator in hand! "Hello – I'm Hector's wife Marilyn." She handed me the part, then held up a small, odd-shaped wrench. "Hector says you'll need this to get it back in."

"Thanks – I wasn't sure I left it at the right house."

"You didn't," she laughed, "but Calum brought it down to us." Marilyn gave me the bill – I was surprised at the small amount. "You can pay Hector when you bring back the spanner." With a cheery wave of the hand, she was off.

Peter Drake is a local fisherman – one of the best – yet from his speech you'd know he is clearly English. He came to the Northwest Highlands as a child, spending his school holidays on property owned by his grandfather. Peter is intelligent, his family has money, and he could have made a comfortable life down in England. Instead he chose a different, harder existence. He had fallen in love with Coigach, the mountains and the sea, and more especially a bonnie dark-eyed lass named Sally. They married and settled in Polbain, and Peter bought the *Sea Swallow* and cast his future on the dark waters of Loch Broom.

The cold clear depths are teeming with life, attracting large trawlers which fill their holds with fish by the ton. But closer inshore, local fishermen in smaller boats can still make a living by setting creels, or traps, for lobster and prawn. Peter fishes prawns in deep water from early spring through summer, and lobsters in shallow rocky holes around the islands in the winter. The months when fishing is down are spent repairing the boat, mending gear and patching holes in the creel netting with shuttles of ancient design.

It is hazardous work, fishing alone, often in tossing seas and rough weather. 'Shooting a fleet' of prawn creels takes strength, organization, good timing – and no little bit of luck. A fleet consists of half a mile of rope with a large float at each end, and 50 net-covered, steel-framed creels strung out along its length. The baited creels are carefully stacked

in sequence behind the *Sea Swallow's* wheelhouse, the polypropylene line looping about on the slippery deck. Peter has to put the boat on a course and open the throttle, then leave the wheel and step out on deck to start 'shooting the fleet' by tossing the first float overboard. As the float bounces away in the wake, he has to throw the creels after it one by one, while the long blue line runs out around his boots and goes slithering over the stern. Should he become tangled in the line, he'd be dragged overboard and into the depths by the weight of his own fishing gear. And there would be no one on board to notice.

Lifting a fleet is less dangerous. Peter recovers an end float and loops the line over *Sea Swallow's* hydraulic winch. Like seats on an alpine chair-lift, the creels come up one by one to debouch their cargo. The catch is tossed into a fish box, and the creels carefully stacked again in consecutive order. Back in harbor, he weighs the catch to gauge its worth before trucking it off to market in Ullapool.

It's a hard job, but Peter Drake is good at it. Prawns – also called scampi, Dublin Bay prawns or Norwegian lobsters on the better menus of the world – fetch good prices, and creel-caught prawns are considered the best. Loch Broom lobsters are also superb, and crabs and scallops add to the value of the fishery. A man can keep a family well if he works at it, as many in Coigach do.

Peter tells a story about old Murdo, back in the days when he was fit and partnered at the fishing with Donnie Shaw. Lobster prices had jumped high in the market, so the two bachelor crofters were eagerly tending their creels off the Summer Isles. Murdo was gingerly taking a nice fat lobster from a creel when the crustacean clamped a powerful claw onto his thumb. Murdo cried out in pain and struggled to pry the claw open. "Tear it off!" shouts Donnie, "Tear it off!"

"Not at fourpence the pound" Murdo returns through clenched teeth.

# Dipping

It was one of those rare autumn mornings when the horizon was clear and the Dundonnell mountains across Loch Broom looked deep blue and close. Barb and I had been living in Castlehill for a month and more, but today was my first real opportunity to get to know my neighbors, for it was the day of the autumn sheep dipping. Twice a year, every sheep in the Highlands has to be immersed in a chemical bath to protect them from blow-flies, ticks, lice and other parasites.

Eight or ten men from Coigach's scattered crofts had gathered at the Polbain fank, a set of sheep-sorting pens below Murdo's cottage. Donnie Darling I recognized, of course, and Ian Roll, captain of the fishing-and-tour boat *Hectoria*. Another I knew by reputation only: Alasdair West of Achnahaird, a burly man of middling height, jovial face and an air of quiet authority. Several others I had not met before, but there were no introductions when I came down to the ramshackle wooden pens of the fank. Just polite nods.

Over a hundred North Country Cheviots were bunched against the fence at the far end of the fank, looking surly and suspicious; the men joked quietly amongst themselves as they eyed the sheep. Wilf, wearing yellow oilskins, was using a push broom to stir the dark creosote stinking chemicals in the concrete trough of the dipper. No one seemed to be organizing things, no one gave directions or instructions. Men stood around, rolling cigarettes thinner than drinking straws that smoldered when lit and died to paper stubs in the corners of their mouths.

With no apparent signal, the crofters began moving forward, herding the reluctant ewes toward the end of the pen where a narrow gate stood above the end of the dipper. As each sheep was forced into the opening, big Ian Roll grasped it by the fleece and launched it into the trough, where Wilf pushed it completely under with his push broom. By the time it scrambled up a ramp into the adjoining pen, the sheep's eyes, nose and mouth were burning from noxious chemicals, its wool was saturated. And it no doubt felt confirmed in its opinion that human beings are not to be trusted.

When the last of the soggy sheep were turned free to the hills again, Donnie Darling invited me to join him at Am Fuaran, the pub two miles up the road at Altandhu. It was here that I was initiated into the tradition of rounds. It began innocently enough, when the two of us entered the bar. Donnie, whose sheep had been the beneficiary of our efforts, bought a couple of whiskies. Blended Scotch whisky, of course, served up in a small glass with just enough space for a splash of plain water – the standard dram in these parts.

The pretty young woman behind the bar handed me the dram. "Are you up on holiday?"

"No, my wife and I are renting a house in Polbain."

"Oh," she smiled. "You're the Americans in Castlehill." She knew. Very little happens in Coigach that isn't soon known by everyone.

I had barely consumed that first dram from Donnie when another appeared at my elbow. Round two, courtesy of another man from the Polbain dipping who had joined us. My companions tipped the whisky glasses with mutual mutterings of 'slainte mhath' and 'slainte mhor." The first is pronounced SLAN-CHA VAH, Gaelic for "good health"; the traditional response SLAN-CHA VOR is "great health."

In the glow of their generosity, I had to reciprocate with round three – a larger round, for now there were five of us at the bar. No matter. And even as I sipped at that third whisky, two more men came in to celebrate the dipping at the fank. Rounds four and five crossed the bar and soon disappeared. I think I bought round six, but can't remember how many whiskies, or for whom.

I stood at the bar in a swirl of cigarette smoke and whisky, surrounded by conversations I barely understood and men I hadn't met. Yet I had worked with them, or at least tried to work without being too much of a nuisance. And I felt comfortable in their presence. I tried to introduce myself in the typical American way – hi, my name is, and a greeting hand thrust forward. From their puzzled reactions, I might as well have been proffering a dead fish. They already knew who I was. They knew who they were. That was all they needed.

Being a nation of strangers, Americans make first contact in a hurry – exchange names immediately, professions in ten seconds, life histories in a minute. The Highlands are a world of neighbors and clans – when strangers meet, they cautiously probe genealogies for mutual connections. "Och, then you'd be cousin to Morag who lives in Strathwhosis? " "No, to Morag at Glenwhatsis, mother to Hector the piper." "He who has the boat at Ardwhere?" "Aye, 'twas my uncle Hamish who had it before him." "I know the very boat." Linkage made, the questioning ends. If you want to know a man's business, wait until he leaves, then ask someone else – they'll be happy to tell you.

I don't have any idea who won that first bout at the Fuaran, but at the end of the last round I was still standing. Somehow I navigated the winding single track back to Castlehill. And fell into bed at three o'clock in the afternoon.

*Jack had definitely "too much drink taken" and wasn't feeling too chipper tonight. He was sitting by the fire, pretending to read, when round about 9:30 there's a knock on the door. In from the dark sways Donnie-next-door, proclaiming what a great chap Jack is and insisting on opening the bottle he brought.*

By this time the very thought of whisky was repulsive but courtesy forced me to bring out a pair of glasses, and Donnie's courtesy left damn little room in my glass for water to temper the liquor. I sipped slowly at the drink while Donnie sang a few ditties in Gaelic for us; and when he wandered out of the room toward our toilet (which, thank heavens, he found unerringly), I determined to empty my glass. Unfortunately in my muddled state, I hit upon the inspired notion of throwing the volatile liquid into the fireplace.

*The explosion almost knocked me off the hearth where I was sitting, and only a miracle kept my hair from being singed away. There's an amazing amount of power in the whisky up here. Anyway, we finally managed to send Donnie on down the road about 10:30, and I later learned that we were not the last – nor the most sober – people in the village to be honored by his company that night.*

## September 20

*Woke up today to a terrific storm – wind and rain that have lasted all day. Gale force westerlies forced water up under the roof slates, and water coming down from the hill is flooding in along the back walls of the house. The office ceiling leaked a few drips at first, so we put pans on the floor to catch them. But the leaks multiplied and we soon ran out of pans. Jack stuck pins in the ceiling at every leak, and ran threads from each pin down to a central collecting pot. When drops of water run down along the threads it makes them dance a jig – strangely artistic!*

*I am sitting here in our lounge in front of a cheery blaze, while the wind and rain beat against the window. The coal man came today and we bought the first of many bags. We have a stone shed out back where the coal is kept. I've never had a coal fire before – it's nice and cozy and the coal burns longer than wood.*

*October 12th*

*Today I finally got down to painting. This first week will just be doing exercises with color and technique – I won't be doing any actual picture-type painting for quite a while. But every time we go for a walk I see a dozen scenes I'd like to paint – there certainly is no lack of inspiration. I've been trying to get in a couple of hours a day of guitar practice too. I'm making some progress – but it's slow going.*

# The Chicken Race

We buy our eggs every few weeks from Keanchulish House, a farm near Ardmair where they keep several hundred brown hens ranging freely over the hillsides. Normally, whenever we drive through the gate and along the driveway to the farmhouse, the hens stop their pecking and peer down at us for a while, then go back to their feeding. But one time it was quite a different experience.

We had forgotten to call the farm, but decided to stop by on our way back from shopping in Ullapool and pick up a few dozen eggs. Barb was driving, I got out and swung the gate open and shut behind the Mini. As we drove on toward the house, we noticed that hens were running down to the road from the hillsides, coming down in dozens, scores, hundreds! Honking the horn and driving slowly through the gathering crowd, we made it to the house and stopped. No one was in – the people were apparently away on holiday. And their poultry were just as apparently eager to be fed.

We were trapped. Barb couldn't move the car for fear of flattening hordes of chickens, or colliding with ducks or geese which had joined the throng. I had to get out of the car and shoo the clucking multitudes in front of the Mini while she turned it and slowly edged down the hill. We led a noisy avian parade across the narrow plank bridge, followed by an increasingly indignant population of poultry.

Barb slowed and swung the car door open, but the moment I tried to get into the car the birds crowded around and made driving impossible. Again I got out front and cleared a path, this time running faster in hope of outpacing the pursuers.

Down the road we rushed, me yelling and waving my arms like a madman, scattering chickens, geese and ducks in all directions, Barb driving at my heels, hundreds of hens in hot pursuit. Finally we got far enough ahead that she could slow down, and I leapt into the Mini as she hit the accelerator. Wheels churning gravel, we roared away in a cloud of dust and a cacophony of clucking, making good our escape from the Hungry Hens of Keanchulish.

## October 17th

*The third beautiful day in a row. Jack fixed the washing machine again and we could hang sheets outside and know they would dry. I made whole wheat bread this morning. While it rose we walked down to Joan & Murdo's and Jack regaled them with his escapades at the pub. Joan chided him and Murdo looked wistful. He used to go up to the Fuaran every Saturday. "It's a friendly place", he says. "It's a shame the world can't be more like the Fuaran – friendly."*

*We'd been talking about the woes of the world – somehow it is not "too much with us" here among the islands and the sea, as it was back in the city with the crowds and TV. I haven't missed TV even once – people yes – but the life we had with all the "mod cons" – no!*

# Unrequited Love

When people – especially preachers – talk about the "innocence" of lambs, something in the back of my mind rings an alarm bell. For once, in Coigach, I was almost victimized by a sex-crazed sheep.

As these things do, it all began innocently enough. Our friends Wilf and Wendy were planning to go away on holiday, and asked if Barb and I would "sit" their little flock of pet sheep for two weeks. "There's nothing to it, really," chirped Wendy. "Mostly, they'll be up on the hill eating grass. Just put out a bucket of food for them once a day."

"Aye," said Wilf, "but mind Freddie doesn't eat it all himself, the cheeky devil – you'll do better with two buckets..."

"We've plenty buckets," she added. "You can have one for each of them, just to keep it fair."

"And we'll give you a bag of those nuggets."

"Oh, they do love their nuggets. Just keep a few in your pockets and they'll be eating out of your hand."

"You'll hardly know they're there, Jack," Wilf beamed.

*W&W brought the sheep up this afternoon. They are off to England for a fortnight to visit family – and we are to keep their sheep from being bored and give them water and oats. W&W act like parents leaving their children behind. Last I saw of the sheep tonight there was one lying on each step in front of the house. They've all blown up like balloons chomping on the long green grass in the yard.*

For the first few days, all went well. The sheep grazed happily on the slope below Castlehill, ignoring us as we came and went during the day, crowding eagerly around us when the feed buckets came out. The only inconvenience was their choice of resting place on the front steps. We had to dodge, wade and push our way through the livestock to get to our front door. Duck inside quickly and slam the door to prevent them from cheerfully following us in. And take off our wellies, which kept picking up evidence that their digestive tracts were in good order.

But one morning, something changed in Frieda. Maybe a hormone kicked in. She had never been wooed and won – Wilf had always sequestered his little band of sisters when the breeding rams called 'tups' were abroad in Coigach at year's end. So she didn't know exactly what it was she suddenly yearned for. But yearn she did. And her little ewe's heart began beating for me.

I first noticed the problem when I came down for breakfast.

"Ba-a-aa-a-aa!" There was Frieda, her nose pressed against the kitchen window, her tail spinning wildly.

"Ummm – what's she after?"

"I don't know." Barb poured the tea. "Maybe she's hungry."

"Ba-aa-a-aa!" The voice more insistent now.

"It isn't feeding time yet. She sounds distressed. I'll take a look." I started to open the back door, and the ewe charged at me. I leapt back and slammed the door. "God, she's gone aggressive!" I peered out the window, trying to see if there was anything wrong with her. She peered in, yellow eyes fixed on me, tail still spinning. "She looks okay – just acting odd."

Frieda kept up her end of the conversation throughout our breakfast. Whenever I spoke, her tail spun; when Barb spoke, it was still. And after, when I went out to work at the typewriter, she raced around and pressed her big nose against the office window. "Ba-aa-a-aa!" I got up and stepped into the lounge. "Ba-aa-aa-aa-aa!" Everywhere I went in the house, there was Frieda calling at the nearest window, persistent as Mary's little lamb.

Later in the morning I went out to run some errands. Frieda was at the front door. I had to force my way past her, and she chased me down to the gate. The other sheep ignored us and continued grazing. When I returned, the bunch had moved up the hill toward the back of the house, but Frieda's head shot up when I came into the yard, and she came joyfully down to greet me. She butted her head against my hip, and tried to cut me off as I climbed toward the house. I had to shove her back hard to get the door closed behind me, and she cried forlorn on the doorstep.

For the next few days, Frieda stalked me. At the gate. At the doors. At the windows. Where I went, she went. At the sound of my voice, her tail spun. She paid no attention to Barb. Or to anyone else who came to Castlehill. I alone was the object of her affections, and this was one true-hearted ewe.

Now, a little attention from the opposite sex is always flattering. And a man couldn't ask to be mistaken for a more macho creature than a breeding tup, whose melon-sized testicles can service a dozen females without even noticing. But Frieda's intentions had become all too obvious, providing endless amusement to Barb, to the neighbors, to everyone but me.

The fourth day of Frieda's love siege was cold and windy, a day when we needed every bit of heat to fend off the chill from Castlehill's thick stone walls. "The coal bucket's empty," Barb reminded me.

"Oh." I knew the ewe was lurking outside somewhere. "Uh – would you mind getting it?"

"Can't – I'm in the middle of this." She was kneading bread dough.

I picked up the coal bucket and tiptoed to the kitchen window. No sign of Frieda. Gingerly, I slid the bolt, pushed the back door open and peered out. No Frieda. The tumbledown stone shed was only a few steps away. I eased silently into the narrow passageway between old wooden boxes, barrels and coils of rope. Gray light filtered in through holes in the walls, barely reflecting off the black pile at the back of the shed. I put down the bucket, picked up a shovel and bent forward to thrust the steel blade into the coal.

That's when Frieda got me. Approaching silently, she rammed her big hot nose into my backside and thrust her passionate weight against me. I dropped the shovel and wheeled around. The ewe's woolly girth filled the passageway, trapping me. And she wasn't about to back out. I sensed, in the darkness, that she was smiling. "Ba-aa-aa-a!"

I braced my hands on barrels on either side and vaulted over her back in a mad scramble to flee. Before Frieda could turn around, I was out in the open, into the kitchen and leaning breathless with my back against the door. Barb had watched the whole drama, from stalk to escape, and her gales of laughter blew away in tatters whatever was left of my male dignity.

The wind died down that night, and it was quiet next morning at breakfast. Unusually quiet. Outside the kitchen window, birds flitted in the rowan tree. No sheep in sight. I went out to the front of the house. Wilf's sheep were grazing in the yard, Frieda among them. I stepped outside. Fred and Barabel looked up for a moment, then went back to their munching. Frieda never looked up, or said a word to me. Nor did she ever again.

In a way, I felt a little – well – rejected.

## October 24th

*Murdo gave Jack an old copy of the Ross-shire tourist magazine that had a cover photo of Murdo shearing a sheep – he used to be quite good at it. He was a handsome man at that time – only about eight years ago – strong and capable. It must be terrible for him now to be so weak and sick. I am working on a painting of that scene to remind us of what he used to be.*

# Elec-Centricities

If you're at all like me, you think of electricity as something useful that comes out of two little holes in the wall. You know that electrical appliances are made to plug into those two little holes. And you assume that as long as you keep your fingers out of light sockets and your butter knife out of the toaster, electricity is benign and reliable. These beliefs have held more or less true throughout our lives. Not so in Coigach.

Within living memory, many remote areas of Scotland were not served by electric power. Even after the end of World War II, heating and light in some Highland homes depended on peat, coal,

candles, and paraffin – what Yanks call kerosene. It wasn't until
the late 1940s that the intrepid engineers from North of Scotland
Hydro-Electric, working in the wild mountains through storms and
snows, began setting poles and stringing wires across the immense
spaces of Wester Ross.

So electricity was a latecomer to Coigach. And has never felt quite
comfortable being there. Thus power outages can be frequent and long,
especially during the wild storms and gales of (choose any month). This
is a serious problem in our upstairs bedroom, in which the sole source
of warmth is a small 'electric fire' of feeble performance. In the damp
chill of (choose any season), night creeps in on heavy, frozen limbs
and overlays the bed like a sullen glacier. The electric under-blanket,
normally turned on an hour before retiring to make the bedding toasty
warm, becomes useless when starved of its life-giving current.

On nights when the power fails we have learned to dress for bed
– thick woolen socks, trousers, cable-knit sweaters and knit wool caps
are the norm. Barb likes to wear wool gloves as well. All this bulky
clothing makes for a friction fit beneath the blankets, so that turning
over is well nigh impossible. Thus encumbered, we huddle together
through the long dark night – unless the power happens to come back
on at 2:30 a.m., in which case the electric fire glows with a vengeance
and we awake overdressed and steeped in sweat.

Even when the power is on in Coigach, it isn't the most convenient.
In America, one buys an electric appliance, brings it home and simply
plugs it in. Not so in Castlehill, as we discovered shortly after moving
in. We had driven over the mountains to Inverness, just to buy Barb
an electric hair dryer at Boots the Chemist. She wanted to use it in
the bathroom when she washed her hair. But when we got home and
opened the box, we discovered that there was no plug at the end of
the cord – just bare wires! Was this a faulty product? No – just an
accommodation to the fact that residential electricity has many faces
in Britain.

Wall sockets and their matching plugs come in many forms here.
Two small round prongs. Two large round prongs. Three small round
prongs. Three large round prongs. Three small square prongs. Three

large square prongs. Don't ask me why – perhaps it is a job-creation scheme by the electricians' union. But short of making every electric appliance with an octopus of tangling cords, manufacturers simply omit the plug and leave you with bare wires dangling. It's up to you to fit the correct plug.

So – which plug is correct? It depends. In an apparent fit of enthusiasm, whoever first installed electricity in Castlehill tried every different socket configuration possible. No two rooms are wired alike. There are two varieties of triple-prongers and a large double round socket scattered about the kitchen alone. The trick, then, is to determine exactly where you expect to use the appliance. In the case of the new hair dryer, Barb's obvious first choice was in the bathroom.

But wait – bathrooms in the UK don't have electrical outlets. Perhaps back in 1888 some toff in London dropped a lamp in his bathtub and expired; whatever the reason, Brits have ever since been chary of electricity in the loo. Even the light switch is usually outside the bathroom door – a fact visiting Americans realize after banging their shins on the toilet bowl while groping in the dark for a wall switch. So you have to choose some other place for your hair dryer. Make note of the wall socket configuration. Then make another trip into town to purchase the right kind of plug for it.

There are, of course, dual-purpose plugs which can be modified to fit – converting round prongs to square or vice versa. There is even a universal plug – about the size and weight of your common hand grenade – which has at least 27 moving parts and can be adapted to any wall socket known to man with the aid of an engineering tool kit in less than two hours by following three pages of instructions carefully, if all goes well. Assuming that halfway through the process your wife doesn't decide she'd rather dry her hair in the kitchen, which has a different type of socket from the bedroom which had been her second choice.

The upshot is that every electrical appliance has its own special socket in its own special room. Mind you, just attaching the right pattern of prongs and plugging it in won't guarantee you results. You have to know the other part of the equation. Behind the couch, beneath a table or back of the umbrella stand, every secretive wall socket has its own fuse, and its own switch, and often have I cursed an inert appliance without realizing that I had forgotten to turn the current on at the wall.

Not only are the sockets fused, there is also a fuse board for the whole house. In Castlehill, the fuse box is in the kitchen. But it isn't a box. It is a wooden board mounted up near a corner of the ceiling. No convenient circuit breakers, no clamps for buss fuses, not even sockets for screw-in fuses. Just exposed electrical contact posts connected by short lengths of twisted-on bare wires. The householder is expected to stock cards of 5-, 10- and 15-amp fuse wire, ready to be cut to length and wrapped between the appropriate posts. Replacing blown fuse wires scares the hell out of me, because it combines all my worst fears: standing on a wobbly wooden chair (acrophobia), figuring out which wire goes from where to where (technophobia), and actually sticking my fingers into the damn thing (electrophobia).

My paranoia was not unjustified. One morning electricity came into the bathroom and tried to kill me. Or at least, threatened me. I was filling the sink with water and was about to wash my face. My right hand was on the cold water tap. I put my left hand into the water. And immediately felt an electric current running through my arms. Yike! I pulled back. Literally, shocked. But that's impossible!

Gingerly I dipped my hand into the water – it was okay. I withdrew the wet hand and touched a cautious fingertip to the faucet. No problem. Perhaps it was my imagination. I laughed at myself, thinking of the deranged character in Robert Service's Ballad of Pious Pete, who imagined a neighbor was persecuting him: "But I killed the galoot when he started to shoot electricity into my walls." Ha ha! What nonsense!

I returned to my ablutions. Yike! Somehow, an electric current had sneaked into the plumbing and was looking to ground itself through my tender body. It was a small current, true – more of a tingling sensation than a real shock – but real nonetheless. And who knows how it might grow, and manifest itself again? Carefully avoiding contact with the bathtub, unwilling to even pee in the toilet, I threaded my way out of the bathroom and down to the kitchen. Barb was about to fill the electric kettle for tea.

"Stop!"

"What?" She turned, puzzled.

"Don't do that! Don't touch the faucet!"

"Why not, for heaven's sake?"

"It's electric!"

Barb stared at me wide-eyed, convinced that the inevitable had finally happened – I'd gone completely bonkers. Okay, maybe there was a touch of hysteria in my voice. But after I explained the problem twice (she'd been more than a little skeptical the first time), she calmly suggested that I phone the Hydro office and report the problem. And after very cautiously touching the phone, just in case...that's what I did. The person at the other end of the line took my report with the phlegmatic professionalism of a bomb squad dispatcher. Sorry about that, old chap, we'll see what can be done.

The Hydro crew showed up later that day and went around Polbain doing whatever they do with probes and meters and testing thingies. Turns out that a fault somewhere down near Morag's house was feeding current into the saturated peaty soil, and thence through our water lines. They fixed it, packed up their whatevers and left. Calm returned to Castlehill.

But I never again approached that bathroom sink without just a wee bit of trepidation.

## November 3rd

*Jack is finally getting down to some serious writing in the early morning hours, and I have started to do some painting. I get so caught up in it that I lose all track of time and Jack has made dinner several times last week rather than interrupt my concentration. It seems that there are not enough hours in the day to do everything we need to do.*

## Nov. 10th

*Today I finished my first painting – a copy of the old 1820 print of Tanera pier which I found in Fraser Darling's book "Island Farm."*

*I'm quite pleased with it since I know I couldn't find a copy of the original print anywhere. It's all in sepia tones – easier to work with than a full palette – I'll have to ease into color now. I feel I did learn a lot about what is possible to do with watercolor though.*

## November 29th

*Thanksgiving is past – and an eventful one it was. I was feeling a little blue about missing the holiday with my family, so we asked W&W and Joan up for the traditional American feast. We had spent the past few weeks hunting down the vital ingredients in Ullapool, Dingwall and Inverness (canned pumpkin and cranberries, unknown here, had to be smuggled in from the States). I was up early Thursday morning starting the giblets boiling and making pumpkin pies. Twenty minutes after the pies went into the oven, the electricity went off. Panic, woe, dismay!*

*I was sitting there in despair with my head in my hands, but Jack gave me one of his typical Pollyanna pep-talks – "Of course we can make Thanksgiving dinner on a one-burner camp stove! We just have to figure out how!" So – I called the Macdonalds next door and arranged for the pies to finish up in their Aga oil stove. We passed them over the fence and when they were done, gave one to our kind rescuers along with cream I'd had to whip with a wire whisk.*

*Wilf offered us the gas oven in the little caravan he rents to summer visitors, so I made dressing, stuffed the turkey, and trekked it half a mile down the road – and all afternoon Jack was driving back and forth to baste and check its progress. Meanwhile, I cooked what I could in advance on the camp stove. The one casserole was carried back and forth to our neighbors' Aga and the rolls and pie were warmed in front of the bottle-gas heater in our kitchen. At 3:00 it was getting dark so we set out candles and two lanterns for light, and got the fire going in the lounge.*

*Jack collected the turkey from the caravan, and it was a most beautiful dark brown. Wilf, Wendy and Joan arrived in their Sunday best – and after a final flurry of activity we sat down to a dinner of turkey, dressing, mashed potatoes, gravy, broccoli and water chestnuts, candied carrots with almonds, cranberries, pumpkin pie and coffee – all done to a turn. Afterward we had a lovely evening around the fire. And as our guests were leaving...the power came back on, just in time for the electric heater upstairs to make our bedroom warm and cozy. It was the most terrible wonderful Thanksgiving I've ever had.*

# Winter

## Early Winter

Winter has finally come to the West Highlands, and transformed the great brooding mountains and offshore islands into glittering white magic worlds. The snow-covered pines by the bright red gate below Castlehill make a merry Christmas scene, and the occasional sheep wandering by in the background looks like a refugee from a Sunday School pageant.

The snow here comes in quick, dark squalls between breaks of blue sky. At this high latitude – we are as far north as Juneau, Alaska – the sun stays low on the horizon to the south, making daylight a seamless transition from sunrise into sunset through a seven-hour arc of red, orange and pink.

Yesterday I went out with Peter Drake on his fishing boat *Sea Swallow*, to check his lobster traps set around the Summer Isles. Grey sea, black rock, white snow drifting down from blue-grey sky, a monochrome world relieved by bright orange buoys on the sea and Peter's matching oilskins. It was a cold day, but with no wind, so the work of raising and tending the traps kept us warm. And last night Barb and I enjoyed the bounty of the sea once more, in the form of a delicious red lobster washed down by a crisp sauvignon blanc!

We're learning to move to the rhythm of this land and the life of a West Highland fishing and crofting community. I've spent long days working side by side with neighbors as we gathered and sorted, dosed and marked their sheep, and other days fishing on the sea. The locals seem a bit stand-offish at first, but only because they tend to be a bit shy; once we've gotten to know people, they're friendly, great conversationalists, and ideal neighbors.

My writing has been going slowly, but I'm fairly satisfied with what I've done so far. At the moment I have a good excuse to stop working, because my electronic typewriter has gone berserk again and has to be sent off for a cure.

---

## THE MOCCASIN BEAR
### CHAPTER I   NIGHT RAID

It was the lid of the jelly jar that gave the bear away.

She had risen dripping from the dark water minutes before, and made her way across the island with the silent confidence of long ownership. Someone was in her territory tonight, and she moved toward the campsite with a heart full of larceny.

In starlight and a sliver of moon she paused behind a tall red pine to survey the clearing. A pale blue tent crouched against the rim of trees, and aluminum pots reflected thin nightglow by the fire ring. On the great rock slab sloping down to the lake lay the long smooth shape of @n inverted canoe, a single paddle prOpped against its side. And, <areles$ly s+uffed under the bow, a big ruck$a<k held the pr*mise of yet another pre dawn bre@[<f@st. #$&%^!

---

# Benito

To be a journalist, you can't get too involved in your story. You have to be able to step outside of the immediate scene. Hold it at arm's length, analyze it, turn it this way and that, pick it apart, be objective. Even though I once worked at a newspaper, went to a journalism school, and have been a professional writer all my adult life, I never became a journalist.

I get too involved in anything I'm doing. I can't write about it when I'm doing it. That's why the first novel I've been trying to write isn't about what we're doing now, but something we did in the past, in a place far away that has nothing to do with Scotland. It is set in the vast tract of forest, lakes and running rivers that lie along the border between the US and Canada. It is about canoes and bears and portages, and a conflict between those who love the silent land, and those who love only what they can take from it.

So, for a few hours every day, I've been sitting at my makeshift desk in Castlehill, staring out the window at fishing boats chugging past the Summer Isles, at the growing snow mantles atop the dark blue Dundonnells across Loch Broom, and trying to peck out a tale of the canoe country on Benito's key board.

Benito is an electric typewriter. It is Italian. It used to work. But since coming to damp chilly Scotland and the dubious electrics of Castlehill, it has gone into a sulk, and developed a habit of going on strike. I can no longer trust it. Thus Benito.

It's not just that the typewriter doesn't work. Benito is treacherous. He'll play nice for a while, rolling out a sunny sentence or so, maybe a nice, clean paragraph. Then without warning he'll inject a string of raND@m letters into mid-sentence. It can h?ppeN any time, ^nywh#re. At first I thought it was me, but even when I carefully peck out one letter at a time, Benito responds sometimes with gibberish. There is an evil circuit somewhere inside him, and I lately determined to exorcize it.

The nearest repair center for Benito's brand is a good five hours over the mountains to the south, down below the Great Glen and Glen Coe, over the Rannoch Moor and past the bonny banks of Loch Lomond, in the Victorian city of Glasgow. The distance and the lovely drive made perfect excuses for a few days' getaway from Coigach to the bright lights of the big city. We dropped Benito off with a hopeful benediction; the repair people said they'd ship Benito home in a week. We checked into a B&B just off Sauchiehall Street and found a good Indian restaurant for supper. Next day we shopped among unaccustomed crowds in the bustling city, and that night took in Tosca at the Theatre Royal. Driving home, I looked forward to a week without Benito, and without the guilt that drives me to write.

As promised, Benito returned. And with a vengeance. Although the shipping box looked fine, the transformer inside had been damaged, and the t%pewr[ter was, if anything, w@rse than before. My phone call to the repair shop was sulfurous, but their response was more than accommodating. "Bring it back down and we'll make good on it." Okay – another two day journey to Glasgow.

We dropped Benito off with a malediction. The service technician said it might take another week or so to find and correct the problem. But meanwhile, he offered to send us home with an old but functioning manual typewriter. I realized that meant I wouldn't have an excuse not to write, but I couldn't refuse the offer. Not with Barb there.

A week later, the typewriter technician called. As best I could sort out his glottal Glaswegian accent, he was reporting that Benito is beyond their power to cure. Did I want him to ship the remains home? I almost suggested an indecent place of interment, but resisted the temptation and said any dumpster in Glasgow would suffice. He said I was welcome to keep the old manual typewriter, which I gratefully accepted.

The keys might stick occasionally, but at least when they do I can pry them apart. I could learn to trust a machine like that.

## Dec. 4th

*I'm finally finishing the portrait of Murdo shearing a sheep. I used Tanera and the islands as the background and the painting has come out rather well I think. I plan to frame it and give it to Joan and Murdo. I spend hours every day now in my studio – the time just flies by.*

## December 8th

*Today I made three kinds of Christmas cookies – while the snow fell outside our kitchen window. The wind and gales have been replaced by the most wonderful weather. Sunday was warm and sunny so we took a picnic and went to the top of the hill behind our house. We looked out at Lewis and Harris 30 miles to the west – the mountains and cliffs looked close enough to touch! We could see the Storr summit at the tip of Skye 50 miles away to the south – the air has never been so clear!*

*We went into Ullapool yesterday and ordered our Christmas tree from the ironmonger's shop. It seems strangely impersonal to order an over-the-counter tree. We have always gone out to cut our own Christmas tree, and Jack always fumes because I'm so fussy in choosing just the right one. Now we'll get this one sight unseen – supposedly five to six feet tall – for about £4. The Scottish Forestry Commission cuts all the trees, and we're supposed to pick ours up in Ullapool about a week before Christmas.*

Barb's been doing a lot of watercolor painting, and I really like what she's doing. She's also baking all of our bread, which in part may account for my being invited to play Santa – her baking's doing terrible things to my physique!

We're going down to London in a few days for a brief respite from the Highlands – going down to stare at the tall buildings and the heavy traffic and the crowds of people at Christmas season, just to remind us of why we chose to live up here. We find that we don't miss Minneapolis at all – not our house, not the city, not the concerts, not even the dining at the Sofitel. But even though we are surrounded by new friends and good friends here in Scotland this special season, we do miss our family and old friends very much.

# First Christmas Tree

Came a knock at the door. There on the threshold stood Hamish – a big friendly teenager fast becoming bigger – with what appeared to be a sprig of pine in his fist. He grinned as he thrust it forward. "Your Christmas tree, Jack!"

It must have been the sorriest little tree in the forest that year. It wasn't even a native Scots pine, but rather one of those nondescript species grown in vast government plantations that smother the natural moors of the Highlands. A Charlie Brown sort of Christmas tree, a mere stick with a few green branches jutting out, an object for pity more than admiration. It could have served as a coat rack for wood sprites. The young man from Achiltibuie had been shopping in Ullapool; the clerk at the ironmonger's had mentioned our tree and Hamish volunteered to bring it to us.

We swallowed our disappointment, thanked Hamish for his kindness and brought the dismal shrub into the house. I thumped the butt of the little pine on the hard floor of the hallway, as one did with pre-cut trees from holiday lots at home, hoping to shake out the branches a bit. But they were already as out as they'd ever get. Whatever we were to make of our first Christmas far from home, this scraggly pine was where we'd have to begin.

Murdo has told us that in his time, Christmas had not been celebrated in Castlehill, and that no tree had ever been brought into the house and decorated. The Roman church had introduced Christ into the December festivities rather late in the game – the heathens got there long before. There is no known record of Christians celebrating the Nativity until early in the fourth century. And it was probably no accident that it coincided with the Roman festival of Saturnalia and pagan observances of the winter solstice. Most of the traditions we now associate with Christmas – yule logs, candles, decorated trees, gift-giving and general merriment – predate Christianity, coming down from Norse, Roman and Phrygian celebrations timed to the northward turn of the sun.

Until recently in the Presbyterian West Highlands, the celebration of Christmas as we know it was not only ignored; it was shunned. And with good Scriptural reason:

> **Jeremiah 10:2-4** *Thus saith the LORD, Learn not the way of the heathen...for [one] cutteth a tree out of the forest...They deck it with silver and with gold; they fasten it with nails and with hammers, that it move not.*

Now Barb and I were bringing the way of the heathen into Castlehill. While we hadn't any silver and gold to deck our little tree, we did have one short string of colored lights and a bit of Yankee ingenuity. We festooned the tree with white popcorn strung on threads, interspersed with bright red knots of yarn to imitate cranberries. A friend in America had sent crocheted white stars which we dangled amid the sparse branches, along with a few store-bought ornaments. Barb fashioned some origami figures and paper chains out of gift wrapping paper. Inch by inch, we turned the scrawny little pine shrub into a thing of beauty and joy. Fastened it with nails and with hammers, that it move not from its home-made stand. And to make it look taller, set it on a table by the fireplace, ready for the great holiday.

## December 23rd

*Only two days 'til Christmas – I can't believe it! Friday night we went to the pub – all kinds of people were there and we had a good time. Went over to Anne & Iain Campbell's afterward for some singing. Anne Irish is a bright, vivacious young woman from Belfast and one of the few Catholics in this part of Scotland – she was evidently responsible for getting a priest to come over the mountains from Dingwall to say mass in Ullapool (there was no Catholic service before then). Her husband Iain is a good-looking, dark haired local man and a fine singer of Gaelic songs.*

*Today we got up late and I spent most of the day painting. Toward sunset, Joan came in laden down like Santa Claus and gave us two bottles of wine, a chicken for the freezer, two lovely etched glasses from Aileen's craft shop, and a little poem.*

"Och, it's just a few wee things to cheer you up," she said, taking Barb's hands in hers and looking concerned. "You'll be missing your family and friends in America." She looked around the room where she had lived in her school days – a room now festooned with unfamiliar holiday decorations. She gently touched a popcorn string and a paper chain, then a crocheted star on the little tree. Then she nodded. "It's a bonnie tree," she smiled, and her eyes were dancing.

As the light outside faded, I turned on the string of colored lights and we three sat down by the fireside for tea, and sherry, and home-baked cookies. Murdo, though invited, hadn't felt up to coming; perhaps it was his illness, perhaps discomfort at the thought of celebrating heathen ways. But while Joan herself had never before celebrated Christmas in Castlehill, nor done so in her own home, she was as merry as we were that starlit winter evening.

## December 26th

*Here it is Boxing Day already! We've had a busy and delightful Christmas season so far. Tuesday afternoon Jack played Santa at the Children's Christmas party in the Achiltibuie Village Hall. He had problems with the beard falling off – but otherwise it went pretty well, although some of the children were puzzled by Santa's funny accent.*

*Thursday was Christmas eve. We finished wrapping gifts and took a walk since the day was warm and sunny. Later in the afternoon I went to services at Mrs. Longstaff's with W&W. They came over afterward for eggnog and dinner. I had made croissants and they came out amazingly well. After they left we sat by the fire and opened presents, and at midnight called the girls. It was good to hear their voices.*

*Friday – Christmas day – dawned bright and beautiful again. We had our traditional breakfast and I played Santa for opening the gifts. Afterward we went over to Joan & Murdo's to visit and deliver their gift and we had a sherry with them before we went into Ullapool for mass. The drive was so beautiful with the snowy mountains all around. Met numerous friends along the way and stopped to say Merry Xmas. Wendy put on a beautiful turkey dinner and Christmas pudding and we spent a lovely afternoon visiting – then came home to make more phone calls.*

*At 7:00 we went over to Anne Irish's for what turned out to be a fantastic ceilidh! All sorts of people, and everyone contributing to the entertainment. Father Brady, the visiting priest from Dingwall, sang song after song – quite a few Glasgow ballads and "The Orange Flute" (a very anti-Catholic Irish song) and we all sang, played charades and danced until 2:00 a.m. when we tore ourselves away. There was a beautiful bright star over Tanera that night. It was a wonderful Christmas – one I'll remember for a long time.*

## December 30th

*Last night was the big pantomime performance. The Village Hall was packed with people. It was delightful – a take-off on Cinderella called "Bucharella" (which in Gaelic means cow-pat). Poor Bucharella had to do the dipping and shearing and gathering while everyone else went to the Ceilidh where the new laird was to choose a wife. Ann Ha'penny played Bucharella, the Pudding played Fairy Liquid (a popular dish detergent brand), Annie Boysie was the wicked stepmother, Simon Schoolbus and Donnie Post made for truly ugly stepsisters. Ali Beag played a Pakistani Laird and Willie John played the Manager – an absolutely masterful performance!*

*The olio segments between acts consisted of two people dressed as sheep telling silly sheep jokes. During the party scene Ali played his accordion, three young pipers played a medley, and the generously padded ugly stepsisters sang 'These Are Our Mountains' (with appropriate gestures). The whole thing was brilliant, put together by Kenny and Marlene School.*

*After the panto we adjourned to the pub for a pint before the dance. There were a lot of strangers there – one group playing fiddle, guitar, mandolin, concertina and penny whistle. We went back to the hall about 11:30 and danced until 3:00 a.m. There is no alcohol allowed in the hall – but everyone brings a bottle and drinks in the kitchen or out in the parking lot. The older children come and help*

*– in the wee hours they were passing sandwiches around. It seems strange to have children where adults are drinking – but the kids seem to be included in everything here, the old people as well, and there is a strong sense of community.*

*This evening Lance stopped by with some Christmas cookies to decorate our poor tree, and half a salmon of uncertain provenance. He was waiting for Di to pick him up after work. Tomorrow is her last day at the hotel where she milks and tends the animals and works in the garden. She wants a house and land, her animals around her and a place to grow garden crops.*

*Today was fairly warm with a stiff wind from the east. Clouds were heavy on both sides but there was no snow. Jack climbed up on the roof yesterday to patch the places he felt might be the source of leaks (we shall see) and we took the ladders back to Wilf this afternoon and stayed for tea (Christmas cake and cookies) and talked about the panto.*

## December 31st

*New Year's Eve. We had a lovely turkey dinner at Peter and Sally's next door and were there until midnight. Talk turned to Murdo and stories about him before his stroke.*

*Peter said Murdo used to corner people against a wall in the pub, lean against it with one hand, pin his victim nose to nose and complain endlessly about the weather, his health, and so on. One day at the Summer Isles Hotel, people arriving at the pub found that they had to step over Murdo's prone body stretched out in the doorway. Naturally, comments were made about the apparently unconscious man and his disgraceful condition. Suddenly Murdo's eyes popped open. "Well," he said, getting up, "now I know who my friends are," and out he walked.*

# Ways and Byways

## Hogmanay

Now, after a fairly sedate Christmas and a mellow New Year's Eve, comes the riotous time of Hogmanay! It is a joyful and vigorous celebration of the winter solstice that contradicts everything you thought you knew about 'dour' Scots, a week-long marathon of hospitality and celebration that demands stamina, perseverance and a hardy stomach.

No one here seems to know what 'Hogmanay' means or where the word comes from – one guess is the Gaelic oge maiden, which I'm told means 'new morning.' Whatever it means, Hogmanay is the ultimate Highland holiday. Through the first week in January, everyone in Coigach is busy 'first-footing' everyone else. This is a ritual celebration of the first time you put your foot across someone's threshold after the New Year begins.

Murdo tells us that originally, the first person to cross a threshold after the New Year was thought to shape the fortunes of that household for the next twelve months. The best luck came if it was a 'dark man' – dark hair, that is – and handsome. It was also traditional for the visitor to bring a lump of coal or peat to warm the host's hearth.

Nowadays, the lump of coal is more than likely replaced by a half-bottle of whisky or some home-baked treats. When visitors come into a house, the host is expected to welcome them with a warming dram and a cheery toast to the coming year – after that, they provide their own drink, and entertainment as well. If there's a fiddle, guitar or squeezebox in the house, it's likely to be played. Visits can be short or long, but the singing of 'Auld Lang Syne' usually signals that it's time to move on.

There is no such thing as a quiet night at home. If the house lights are on, it's an open invitation to any passing visitor. All night, lines of car headlights stream around the single-track as the younger people go from house to house, seeking gatherings where music and singing are going on. All day, the older folk are visiting friends and neighbors where the ritual drinks and toasts are often followed by restorative tea and cakes.

Outsiders may think of Hogmanay as little more than a drinking marathon. But it is more – a lot more. It is a tip of the hat to the sun's return, a gesture of hope for the year to come, a touching of neighbor to neighbor and friend to friend. Everyone takes part, no one is forgotten.

## January 10th

*Since New Year's Day we've had wild easterly gales – the power went out for a night and a day and the salmon cages at Tanera were damaged again. When it started to blow we were out all night at various Hogmanay parties. The next night we were talked into going to a party at Anne Irish's (they didn't know about it!) by Ken the Bread – a Liverpool transplant and occasional world traveler who lives alone next to W&W in a tiny caravan with no water or electricity. He usually leaves in winter to wander in warmer climes – but this year he chose to stay here. Now that the wind is howling and rain is pelting down, he wonders why he isn't basking in the Carribean sunshine.*

## January 12th

*Today is the Old New Year – celebrated by the old Highlanders. Went to whist last night and learned that Sandy Boots lost about 10,000 salmon when the cages in Tanera anchorage were damaged by bad easterlies right after New Year. A disaster for him and the salmon farm – I don't know if they can recover.*

*I also found out who dresses the strange little doll (she's got only*

*1 eye) perched in the old boat by the roadside at the edge of Polbain. We saw her two years ago when we first came here. Jim Muir said he found her in the sea and threw her into his boat. Lyon White dresses her – changing outfits to suit the season. And so she sits, arm raised as if greeting anyone coming into the village.*

# Deep Winter

Now comes the closed-in time in Coigach. From the first sleety gales of late October through the dark and storm-wracked winter to the first warming suns of Eastertide, the outside world shuns the little community. The welcoming 'B&B' signs are down, the craft shop closed, the beaches empty. Few strangers venture to follow the sinuous single-track road that loops away from the broad well-traveled lanes of the A835 at Drumrunie, writhing between lonely mountains as far as the Wee Mad Road, then on to the sea at Achnahaird, encircling the Coigach peninsula and snaking down the coast through Achiltibuie to shed its pavement skin at Culnacraig, leaving only a thinly worn trail tailing off across the slopes of Ben Mor.

Day after day, week after week, mostly all that we see are ourselves. Two hundred faces become familiar as siblings when none of them change from month to month. Yet far from being bored or feeling confined, we have found a surprising comfort in the embrace of winter here. Enter a shop, post office or pub, and everyone you meet is already a friend. Pull off in a passing place on the single track to make way for an approaching car, and it is a neighbor who stops, rolls down his car window and offers you a snippet of gossip or even a dram from the glove box. If you do see an unfamiliar vehicle, it is likely a replacement for one you've known that has succumbed to the salt air and dissolved into unusable rust. You'll know the driver, because you have worked and laughed and shared meat and drink with him.

Near solstice time, the sun arcs low over the Dundonnels. Daybreak comes well into the morning hours, and nightfall by mid-afternoon. The winter weeks unroll in a slow rhythm of Monday whist games at the Village Hall, Friday night darts tournaments in faraway villages and weekend ceilidhs in the storm-battered houses of Coigach.

Neighbors exchange books, and recipes, and visits into the long, long evenings. When the peat glow fades and the coals burn low in the grey ash, each midnight brings the BBC shipping forecast with its litany of the sea areas surrounding Britain: "Viking, Forties, Cromarty, Forth, Tyne, Dogger, Fisher, German Bight..." The cultured voice drones wind speeds and wave heights, washing over the drowsy mind like a gentle swell, drowning wakefulness.

## January 14th

*Saturday night we went to the pub for the first time since before the New Year. It was crowded, and when it closed a bunch of people came to our place for our first Castlehill ceilidh! And it was a good one – we sang for about 3 hours – popped corn and drank a bit and everyone had a good time – we ended by all holding hands and singing Auld Lang Syne*

*Sunday Father Brady came in for mass at Anne Irish's, so I went to Polglass for the service, then we had dinner with Anne and Iain, Father Brady, Nessie, and Annie & Boysie from Achiltibuie Stores.*

## January 17th

*Monday is whist night in the Village Hall. There were about 14 people there and they change partners and tables after every hand – so we got to meet and talk to everyone. They're really quite amazing. This country seems to both breed and attract a lot of strong characters – most of whom are articulate and witty and make us feel quite tongue-tied. Yet in their old-fashioned way, only the men are allowed to shuffle and deal the cards. Jim Muir is a cheerful and blatant cheat, laughing as he peers over everyone's shoulder and reads off their cards. It was a lot of fun so we'll be going every week. We took both booby prizes at whist – a clean American sweep.*

*Joy came over Wednesday afternoon and took me to the library, a tiny room in the Village Hall which is open once a week from two to four. The books come from the Ullapool library and are changed every three months – a pretty motley selection all told, but I did find a couple I might enjoy. It's another excuse for people to meet and talk – I get the feeling that the books are incidental.*

# The Village Hall

There are no theaters in Coigach. No restaurants. No bowling alleys or shopping malls, game arcades or coffee shops. Thankfully, no Golden Arches. For entertainment, celebration, lively conversation, gossip, companionship, chance company, or simply to pass the time, Coigach has but three resources: the Village Hall, the Fuaran pub in Altandhu, and a wee pub in the Summer Isles Hotel down in Achiltibuie.

The Village Hall is a long, low wooden shed originally built in 1914. In World War II it served as a drill hall for Coigach's Home Guard, a local militia comprised of crofters and fishermen armed with weaponry more suited to battling bunnies than invaders. This raggle-taggle band was led by Captain Howard Seth-Smith, a retired army officer who had been wounded in The Great War. Now almost 90, Howard and his wife Ailsa live at the south end of Polbain, where the old peat road goes off into the hills from the single track.

Monday afternoon we visited Seth-Smiths. Howard said trying to instill military discipline in Coigach was quite a challenge – seems the Coigach crofters couldn't carry out an order without 15 minutes' argument and discussion first. He told us of one day they were having grenade practice – each man had to go up to the drystone wall, throw the grenade over and flatten himself for the blast. Everyone did fine until our friend Murdo threw his underhand, getting great loft, but not much distance. Luckily it barely cleared the wall (took out the corner). Howard said everyone got up looking deathly pale.

Jim Muir tells of the time Captain Seth-Smith issued German language scripts to his handful of troops: "Hände hoch, oder ich schiesse!" – "Hands up, or I'll shoot!" This was to be recited in a firm voice while pointing a shotgun at any Wehrmacht troops or panzer tanks attempting to land at Achnahaird beach. Jim also says that more than a few of His Majesty's hand grenades were employed to harvest sea trout by moonlight from a pool on the Garvie river.

Having neither suffered nor inflicted casualties beyond the

occasional rabbit or fish, Coigach's Home Guard was disbanded after World War II and their drill hall became a community center. The main room is long and narrow, with a small stage at the far end for visiting entertainments or musicians for dances. Little rooms off to the side contain a cramped kitchen, the little library, and the room used for smaller events like our whist drives.

This last room also serves as a surgery, or medical clinic, once a week when the National Health Service comes to Coigach. Every Wednesday, there's a line of people seated against the wall in the main hall, waiting their turn to see the doctor who drives in from Ullapool. Pregnant women, colicky infants, adolescents with acne, men with infections, old folk with arthritis, everyone with any of the thousand natural shocks that flesh is heir to – all patiently await their turn to be ushered into the smaller room for consultation or examination. No appointment is needed – just show up and join the queue. No one asks how you plan to pay, or photocopies your credit or insurance cards, or tells you the doctor's next opening is five weeks away. It is health care at its best, regular, open, and free.

Teas are held in the Hall, as are regular luncheons for Old Age Pensioners, children's parties at Christmas, pantomimes, traveling entertainments funded by the Highland Arts Council, and lively dances during the holiday season. When it stands empty, the Hall's bare wooden walls, dingy windows and creaking floor make it seem barren and gloomy as the surrounding hills. Yet pack it with a hundred or so Highlanders and visitors, put a wheezing accordionist and dazed drummer on the stage to play the opening strains of "The Dashing White Sergeant" or "Mairi's Wedding," and the place becomes as lively, bright and exciting as the Royal Albert Hall.

There was a time when winters here were darker yet – when life in Coigach was precarious, and people survived the cruel months on little more than potatoes, salt herring and hope. Before television and radio, before global positioning satellites and radar and rescue helicopters, when Coigach fishermen faced the sea alone and Coigach families fended for themselves, then the isolation we cherish now had a killing edge to it. Yet even then the winter nights were often passed in song and story, and every house had a fiddle or accordion or a set of pipes ready to set visiting feet a-tapping, and every man and woman performed a personal 'party piece' for which they were known and appreciated – or at least tolerated. This was the original ceilidh – in Gaelic, simply a visit. Nowadays 'ceilidh' is often used as a label for commercial entertainments aimed at tourists in the Highlands. But the informal ceilidh still thrives in homes across the Scottish diaspora, wherever Scots and their hyphenated descendants gather.

# A Certain Cat

Barb has declared winter her favorite season here (so far). In the brief interludes between gale force winds, raging seas and horizontal sleet and rain, the low-raking sunlight illuminates racing clouds and purple-tinged landscapes that never cease to thrill the heart. Our only problem has been that the header tank for our water heater, up in the attic under the roof-beam, has frozen up a few times. Now I've rigged a 100-watt lightbulb up there to keep the valve warm, so perhaps we can once again count on hot water.

The electric water heater is in the bathroom, but the switch for it is downstairs on the kitchen wall, which may seem a bit odd but is actually quite handy. You see, the heater either has no thermostat, or the thermostat doesn't work. So we're careful to switch it on only when necessary for laundry, after-dinner washups, evening baths, etc. After a while, when we begin to hear the merry bluh-bluh-blurp of water boiling in the heater, we have to switch it off again to prevent it burning out. The insulated tank only keeps the water warm for a few hours, so we have to plan our use through the day.

We now have a part-time cat, which shall remain nameless – Peter Drake next door has had her for eight years and never gave her a name. She's nice and solid, no squishiness about her – beautifully garbed in bright orange and black with white paws and a white bib. An ideal cat because she's affectionate, well-behaved, catches mice (3 so far) and goes home to Peter when she needs to be fed.

# The Irish Stranger

It was not the season for tourists.

He didn't belong there in the Fuaran that Saturday afternoon. Among the rough-dressed locals, fishermen and farmers in rubber boots and thick sweaters, the stranger's neat grey suit, white shirt and blue tie set him apart. But the strangest of all was the fact that he obviously hadn't shaved for three or four days, and the contrast of his white stubbled beard with the neatness of his dress was striking. He had white hair and grey, grey eyes that looked tired, and his hands and his voice were shaky.

Donnie Darling, in the ebullience of whisky, tried to strike up a friendly conversation with the stranger, but the man's answers were short and cold, delivered in a taut Northern Irish accent. Undeterred, Donnie tried again by introducing me as "an Irishman from America." The stranger didn't even took at me. "If he's an American," he said, "he's no Irishman." And he turned away, cutting the conversation off. After that, we ignored the unfriendly and edgy man in the corner of the bar at the Fuaran, and the afternoon went on as they do in this wintry season.

A few days later I happened to stop into the Fuaran at mid-day and met Donnie, Alasdair and Roddy at the bar. "Ye remember that Irishman last Saturday?" says Donnie "The police are looking all over for him. They were up here yesterday asking questions!"

The man was said to have stolen a car in England the week before and driven it up as far as Lochinver, then come down the coast to Coigach. He'd stopped at the store in Achiltibuie and asked directions to the Fuaran, where he said he was to meet three friends. When he got to the Fuaran it was closed, but the owner's wife, Siona, took him in and gave him tea and sandwiches. He asked about his friends, and Siona at first thought he might be looking for Anne Irish and her husband, but he insisted he was looking for three men. Whoever they were, they never appeared.

The Irish stranger stayed about the Fuaran that afternoon and evening, shunning conversation, drinking not too much, waiting for something or nothing.

That night he stayed in one of Murdo William's tourist chalets, and the next morning he left without paying. When Murdo reported this to the police at Ullapool, they came up at once and questioned everyone who'd talked to the Irishman. What he was being sought for, and what he was seeking, we don't know to this day...but Andy and Siona searched the premises of the Fuaran carefully that afternoon for anything that might contain an IRA bomb, and tongues clacked all across Coigach about the Irish stranger.

# Weather

### January 18th

*We were going to the pub last night – got our jackets on – but the wind was so horrible (force 12 – over 75 mph!) we decided to stay home by the fire. Today it's still bad and we have no electricity again. I must say, this wind is getting on my nerves. Peter Drake has had his prawn gear ready to go for weeks now – but no chance with this weather. It's going to be a thin season for the fishermen if this keeps up.*

### January 20th

*The weather is still bad – but Jack helped Peter get his first fleets of prawn creels out yesterday. They got another two fleets out today despite the squalls of rain and snow. They also lifted the first fleet and got a beautiful mess of prawns and we had our first meal of fresh prawns of the year – one was as big as a small lobster and the claws were delicious.*

### Jan. 22nd

*The weather's been pretty bad, but Jack and Peter got out two more fleets and lifted four others. Four stone of prawns and that was pretty good. One of the fleets had been dragged by a trawler and the rope cut and a couple creels smashed. That's the problem with gear out while the big trawlers are still around (their season's been extended 'til the end of January).*

On one of the last days of that stormy month I went out with Peter on *Sea Swallow* to lift a few fleets of prawn creels. Dark clouds were scudding low over choppy seas as we worked. Lurching around on the wet deck to stack the creels was difficult. The wind began to rise. Snow squalls passed. The waves grew higher. Soon the world was a wall of streaming white, the little boat was pitching and yawing, and sheets of spray were slashing over the top of the wheelhouse.

Between the wind, the cold, the waves, and the gyrating deck, work became impossible. Common sense would have us heading in to the sheltered harbor and home for tea by the fireside with our wives. But nature had other ideas.

Even though the sky had been obscured by roiling clouds for weeks, Peter well knew the phase of the moon. Twice in the lunar month, at the half moon, modest neap tides keep the harbor navigable 'round the clock. But at the new moon, and again at the full, 16 foot spring tides rush in and out of Old Dornie, flushing the harbor top to bottom. Boats can only get in or out at certain times. We were just coming on to low tide – there wasn't enough water in Old Dornie to float a teacup. It would be three hours before the returning flood would give *Sea Swallow* enough water to get over the bar.

Peter shouted something at me, but I couldn't hear him over the wind. He spun the wheel and turned the boat through a trough between seas to head downwind. Wave crests lifted the stern and bore us forward, the breaking foam racing along the rails and disappearing into the whiteness ahead. I couldn't see where we were, and had no idea where we were going. Had someone else been at the helm, I might have been terrified. But with Peter, it was exhilarating, because I knew he'd see us safe.

In a few minutes, grey land forms emerged from the gloom. We turned again, lunged across a last rushing wave and dropped suddenly into quieter waters. The wind abated. The snow which had been pelting us now fell gently, white feathers drifting against black rocks, black water. *Sea Swallow's* diesel engine slowed, gasped, fell silent as Peter left the wheelhouse to drop anchor. We were close in under the lee of an island, and, for the moment, we were safe.

Three hours is a long time for two men to stand in a wheelhouse the size of a closet. A wheelhouse with only three sides. A working wheelhouse without heat or seat or comfort. And while we were no longer being assaulted by wind and wave, the winter cold wrapped itself around us all the more. We were dressed for working, not for standing still. Not for waiting. We jammed half-frozen hands in our pockets, hunched against the cold, waited for the tide to turn. And talked quietly about – what else? – the weather.

For city folk, weather is only important on weekends and holidays. It can affect picnic plans, or ski trips, or when to mow the lawn. Phases of the moon are of little interest. In a centrally heated, air-conditioned world, weather is simply something happening on the other side of the glass. Modern people can live and work comfortably and happily in a totally hostile environment. Like the South Pole. Or Phoenix, Arizona. But not in Coigach.

Rain, wind and tide rule every aspect of life here, whether it's fishing, or raising sheep, or simply walking to the shop. If the sheep are wet, they can't be clipped. If the rains are cold, the lambs die. And if winds and tides are against you, as Peter patiently explained, you can't get back into the harbor – no matter how bloody cold you are.

Old-timers here tell me that if you can see the Western Isles from Coigach, it is going to rain. If you can't see the islands, it is raining. Okay, it's a hoary old joke, but all too often, too true. The weather here comes at us from the west, where the Gulf Stream and the Labrador Current collide in a volatile brew of arctic and tropical waters, and the fierce continental winds have three thousand miles of open ocean to gather strength before striking our coast.

So, often as not, the weather here is horrid. For which I am grateful. After all, we have a spectacular coast, gorgeous mountains, lovely islands, sparkling beaches. Were it not for horrid weather, the whole place would have been bought up by rock stars, sheikhs and speculators. Coigach offers five-star scenery on a one-star budget, and I can enjoy it all without speaking German or Arabic – so long as I can live with the weather.

Rain is the worst of it. From September through January, we average about 6 inches of rain a month. But averages mean little. Some days are beautiful beyond belief. Others are like living in a submarine – open the door, and you're soaked. The rain can fall with gentle beneficence, bedewing the heather and gracing the gorse. Or it can come at you with unimaginable, unending malevolence, flooding the roads for days – weeks – at a time, seeking and finding every vulnerable chink in the armor of a house.

It feels as if God had turned on the tap. In America's Midwest where I grew up, rain comes and goes. Here it takes up residence. Every day you get up and say, "It can't keep up like this much longer." But it does. And it doesn't just fall – it comes at you horizontally. You see, we have the winds here, too.

Driven by gale force winds, rain creeps up the roof slates, finds its way underneath, works its way down into the house. With doors and windows shut against the storms, intruding rain becomes the damp. The damp becomes mildew. Silent, sneaking, black and stinking mildew. Given a moment's inattention, it becomes aggressive. I once lost a brown leather glove in Castlehill, dropped it behind the umbrella stand in the front hall. When I found it a week later, it was green. Mildew. It comes with damp. And time.

I looked at my watch. Damn, it was cold in that exposed little wheelhouse! "How long now, do you think?"

Peter smiled. "It's not even slack water yet." Snow was gently whirling in eddies behind the sheltering rocks, but higher up it streaked the dark sky, driven by a shrieking wind. "Give it another hour or so." I felt even colder now.

The damp is a multiplier of cold. And this isn't cold like I knew in Midwest winters – that exhilarating sub-zero cold that stings your face, puts frost on your windshield and decorates the trees with sparkling white crystals. You can see that kind of cold, it's right out there on the surface where you can deal with it. No. Coigach cold is leaden. It settles deep in your bones. It is primeval cold, locked in the stony heart of Castlehill's walls, well beyond reach of the feckless fireside. It is internal cold that can't be relieved by superficial means. Maybe that explains the Scots' fondness for whisky.

But wind is the great arbiter of life here. And of death. Not long after we came to Coigach, force 12 hurricane winds drove a crippled Irish merchant vessel onto the west coast of Britain. On board the *Union Star* were the captain, his wife and two young daughters, and four crewmen. Fighting gusts as high as 95mph, a Royal Navy Sea King rescue helicopter was unable to lift anyone off the doomed ship. A motorized lifeboat was launched from shore, and managed to take off four people before it, too, succumbed to 40 foot waves. Altogether, sixteen people perished in that terrible storm. The lifeboat was never found.

And wind strikes those on shore as well. If you want to know if a man lives on the West Coast of Scotland, look at his car. If he's local, there will probably be a vertical crease in the front fender, an inch or so ahead of the driver's door. It happened when he tried to get out of the car in a gale. The wind ripped the door from his hand, wrenched it past its normal position and jammed the front edge into the fender. The resulting crease is a hallmark of Coigach cars.

Wind even determines day-to-day living conditions inside Castlehill. Being equipped with only a primitive washing machine and a hand-cranked wringer, we prefer to dry our laundry on a clothesline outside the kitchen door on pleasant sunny days. But such days are few and far between, especially in winter. And laundry hung out in gales tends to disappear over the hill. So most days our laundry is dried in the lounge on a wooden rack, placed in front of the fireplace and turned every so often. It is a time-consuming process which also blocks most of the warmth. It's not so much fun, sharing a cozy fire with a bunch of steaming socks.

Walking to the Polbain shop most days means getting wet, but I'd sooner try fending off a grizzly with a pop-gun than use an umbrella in these winds. The fastest way to get across the mountains, from Coigach to Inverness? Open your umbrella, sez Mary Poppins.

Snow, on the other hand, isn't a problem. Unless you need to go somewhere. Whatever snow falls along the coast is soon melted by warmer air off the unfrozen sea, or blown off by the bitter winds. But farther inland, snow can gather in deep drifts where the single-track meets the highway at Drumrunie, barricading Coigach from the outside world. And if the road crew manages to open the way, you may only get a few miles before it's closed again at Strathkanaird. Snow drifts can also choke the road from Ullapool to Inverness, where mountains funnel the worst of wintery weather through the bleak pass of the Dirrie Mor.

White flakes were still dissolving in the black water around us and I was shivering badly by the time Peter consulted his watch and began hauling in the anchor. "I think we can make it back in now." *Sea Swallow's* starter growled and the little diesel clunked into action. We were half frozen, but the wind had dropped a bit, and we had a fairly easy run into Old Dornie. Never – before or since – did land feel so good beneath my boots.

### January 26th

*Yesterday the weather blew up a howling blizzard (a complete white-out) and Jack and Peter had to shelter behind Tanera for a few hours. Luckily Peter has a CB radio in the boat and kept Sally informed on what was happening or I would have been frantic. We had hot tea waiting when they came ashore. I hear the whole of Scotland got hit with the worst storms of the year yesterday – lots of roads closed and fallen trees etc. – but the snow's mostly gone here now.*

### January 28th

*January 25th was Robbie Burns' birthday and it was celebrated for the first time here with a traditional Burns Night supper at the Fuaran. It was a sell-out crowd and a real mix of people. There was music and singing and toasts to lads & lassies & it was fun – but somewhat formal and stilted at first.*

# A Burns Night in Coigach

A Robbie Burns Night celebration?

Not in Coigach. At least, none of the locals can recall such a thing.

In fact, most of them haven't given much thought to Scotland's National Poet since childhood. Back then, they had spent long hours in the village schoolhouse, agonizing over the unfamiliar words, the outlandish sounds, indeed, the foreign tongue of Robert Burns' poems. And most, giving up, would gaze wistfully through the classroom window at the sea, and the islands, and the craggy blue mountains that defined their West Highland world.

Ask a crofter in this faraway corner of Scotland what he thinks of Burns, and he'll assume you mean the silvery streams running down from the hills, through the common grazing lands, to join the sea – hazards in which lambs and ewes occasionally drown.

As for Burns the poet – you might as well talk of Byron or Shelley, or even Henry Wadsworth Longfellow – mere scribblers of English. And English that harsh and colorless foreign language has only taken hold in the village within living memory. To the older Coigach natives, poetry belongs exclusively to the Gaelic tongue they learned at their mothers' side.

But the local publican is an outsider who had come up from Burns country, and he is determined to make his pub an island of culture in the Highland wilderness. So it was that hand lettered posters appeared at every gathering place in the little community late in January, proclaiming the approach of Coigach's first ever Burns Night Supper.

Now, anyone who has survived a West Highland New Year – the marathon week of Hogmanay – knows that the latter days of January are a time for quiet recuperation – and perhaps a few minor home repairs. So some folk in the village were a bit resentful of the publican's innovation. Especially as it hadn't been done first by locals. Still, throughout the chill grey gale battered days of early January, the common thread of conversation was, "Are ye goin' to the do at the Fuaran?" 'Am Fuaran' is the Gaelic for a well spring, or watering place, although precious little water is consumed there.

There are those in Coigach, of course, who saw nothing unusual about a Burns Night: the incomers English or, almost the same thing, Scots Lowlanders who have bought up many of the old empty stone croft houses and fixed them up for holiday and retirement homes.

Doctors and lawyers and civil servants they are, city folk, mostly. Decent people, good neighbors to be sure, though sometimes no more attuned to Highland ways than we are.

It is among these incomers that "Scottishness" has the most appeal. None are silly enough to wear the kilt every day, like they do down in Edinburgh, but many of them affect a few words of Gaelic, and some have even joined the Scottish National Party. So it was inevitable that they'd go for a Burns Night Supper.

And so the big night came.

The Burns Night Supper was convened in the Fuaran's carpeted lounge bar. It is only two steps up from the tile floor of the public bar. But on that special night, the wee tartan curtains in the doorways divided worlds apart.

Above, gleaming tables and soft lighting, well cut tweeds, polished brogues, wine, single malt whisky and bright conversation about the affairs of the great world. Below, heavy smoke and the clump of spattered wellie boots, pints of MacEwans and rounds of Bell's Whisky and rumbling talk about weather, sheep and the fishing.

Upstairs, laird and schoolmaster and local councilman, doctor, solicitor and resident foreigners, pensioned civil servants, people from everywhere but here  and many voices rarely heard within the walls of the Fuaran.

Downstairs, fishermen and crofters, boys from the salmon farm, women from the council houses, day laborers, road crew men, the Fuaran Regulars, in for their nightly pints and drams.

Upstairs, they clapped for a witty speech and raised their glasses to toast the lassies; downstairs, someone patted Rosie on the bum and bought a round of drinks. Upstairs, they applauded a crisp response and toasted the lads; downstairs, Rosie slapped a hand away  then she bought a round.

Upstairs, a solicitor from Edinburgh spoke eloquently to a rapt audience, praising the poet philosopher of Ayrshire. Downstairs, fierce old John Alec growled about the rising cost of overwintering lambs in the Black Isle, while Alasdair West nodded and puffed at the smoldering 'black twist' tobacco in his pipe.

Suddenly the conversations, upstairs and down, were quashed by violent sounds. A whacking punch to a leather bladder brought agonized groans from a set of drones – then an angry shriek from an ancient chanter, as Gillis in full regalia piped his way into the Upper Chamber. Behind came Andy the publican, steaming haggis aloft – stalked intently by his mother in law, armed with crossed knife and fork.

At the head table, a retired police constable gave the "Address To The Haggis" in rich rolling Strathclyde syllables. The upstairs audience applauded. At the public bar, Calum from Lewis told one of his outrageous lies. The downstairs audience groaned.

For an hour, the tinkle and clatter of china and glass, the delicate chatter of worldly discussion floated out through the wee tartan curtains, hovering like silver birds above the homespun rumble of local gossip and the thunk of well thrown darts. And then the music began.

Upstairs, the gathered gentry – and would–be gentry – sang the polite version of "John Anderson My Jo." Down at the bar, wee Donnie Darling draped his arm around the nearest woman and bawled out his perennial party piece – this consisting of the first three lines of "North To Alaska," repeated to the end of his attention span.

Hunched in the far corner of the bar, a scar–faced man sat nursing his dram, eyes half closed, ears half listening to the sounds drifting down from above. Words boiled around him, music swept over him, but he sat apart, alone and quiet.

Yet of all the folk in the Fuaran that night, this shy and gentle man best knows the songs of Robbie Burns  songs belonging, like himself, to a softer land far away to the south of the mountains. He is only a drifter, a laborer, a loner – a man for fixing the faucet and clearing the drain, a man for mucking out the sewer pipe. It is his work, and it gives him the name most folk in Coigach know him by – Sandy Plumber. Sandy lives alone in a broken down caravan at the back of someone's croft. Not the sort, you know, to be Upstairs, even if he'd had the price of a ticket.

Sandy Plumber listened intently, eyes glazed and inward looking, as song followed song from the Upper Chamber, no Gaelic airs to catch the ears of the downstairs crowd, just the rich and sentimental ditties that have made Robbie Burns the Prince of Scottish parlor music.

But gradually the upstairs voices grew louder as they vainly tried to rise above the clamor in the lower bar. The clamor, of course, rose higher yet, for none of the Regulars was about to lose a snippet of gossip for the sake of a song that night. For a while, it seemed there was a contest in decibels as each faction tried to drown out the other.

And, for a moment, amidst the uproar and the billowing smoke, one could almost imagine the ghost of a handsome young lad in quaint old breeks, brown hair curling over a high forehead, hesitating on the steps between the two rooms. His lively dark eyes look above, then below. He cannot decide where he belongs. Poor Robbie Burns ploughman and poet, darling of the Edinburgh salons and reveler of the rough country taverns torn again and forever between Upstairs and Downstairs.

It must have been the ghost of Robbie Burns who stood there that night there's no better way to account for what happened next:

It was just one of those coincidental pauses when everyone takes a breath at the same time – a momentary respite, a lull in the verbal storm. And into the silence came the first notes of yet another Burns song.

But these were familiar notes, even to the locals in the public bar, emerging from their memories of school days long ago; notes leading into a song that was neither Lowland nor Highland, Upstairs nor Down a song that belonged to everyone.

> *"Is there for honest poverty,*
> *That hangs its head and all that,*
> *The coward slave we pass him by,*
> *We dare be poor for all that."*

The first words floated out from above. Then others came in from below, uncertain at first, a line here, a phrase there, the chorus ragged but growing in power, voice joining voice across the barriers, the words only half remembered, but the promise never forgotten.

*"What though on homely fare we dine,*
*Wear homespun gray and all that?*
*Give fools their silk and knaves their wine,*
*A man's a man for all that."*

And rising above them all came a strong, sure voice from the back corner of the bar, putting heart and meaning into every word. Standing with his glass in hand, eyes closed, head high, Sandy the Plumber was singing like an angel.

*"Then let us pray that come it may,*
*(As come it will for all that)*
*That Sense and Worth, o'er all the earth,*
*Shall standard be and all that.*
*For all that, and all that, It's comin' yet for all that,*
*That man to man, the world o'er,*
*Shall brothers be for all that."*

(With apologies to the ghost of Robbie Burns, for adapting his Lowland Scots lyrics to colorless common English)

## February 18th

*The live music scene is looking up around here. We were at the bar in Ullapool's Argyll Hotel last week and ran into a young Englishman whom we'd met in December at the Fuaran. Pete Taylor is a fine singer of folk songs and plays all sorts of instruments. Anyway, he's moving from Elphin – where he's been care-taking a house – down to Achiltibuie next month, where he'll be tending dairy cows and goats for the Summer Isles Hotel. So we can look forward to quite a few good evenings of singing again at the Fuaran – and maybe I can get some guitar lessons!.*

## February 20th

*Cloudy morning – Peter's boat* Sea Swallow *is just chugging past in the channel below Castlehill on his way to his prawn creels – some weather is coming in, probably rain this afternoon, the first less-than-perfect day in quite a while. February has been wonderful so far. We took off yesterday morning and drove up into the hills of Sutherland, then across to the east coast and the town of Tain, a tiny royal Burgh chartered in 1066 with an ancient stone Tolbooth (prison tower) in the center of the business district. Did some shopping, had a bar lunch at the Royal Hotel, then motored down to Nigg, where they're assembling a gigantic oil rig for the North Sea fields – quite a piece of engineering. Stopped in Dingwall at our favorite butcher's to pick up half a dozen haggis for the freezer, then home in the fading light. Temperature was in the 50's all day, bright sky, light winds; hard to believe it's still winter back in Minnesota.*

## March 13

*Just got back from dinner at the laird's – traditional roast beef and Yorkshire pudding – and a tour of Badentarbat Lodge, her studio and paintings. Charmian does beautiful portrait work and has an impressionistic style to her painting. She showed us photos of the lovely Victorian home she lived in as a child. The house is filled with mementoes of Tom Longstaff's adventures – there's a scrimshawed walrus tusk and a beautiful long narwhal tusk in the lounge and bronze Nepalese lions in the dining room fireplace. We spent about three hours talking in the lounge by the fire. Mrs. L is a fascinating person and we enjoyed it immensely. She loves fly fishing and gave Jack some good information – and two days salmon fishing on the Garvie.*

# Spring

## War

### April 7th

*The big topic of discussion these days is the Argentinean invasion of the Falkland Islands. Britain has launched a big naval fleet to go down and try to get them back. There's talk of war – the US is trying to mediate. The vicious infighting of the Labour and Conservative parties here makes our Democrats and Republicans look like a bunch of pussycats. I can't get used to the 'debates' in Parliament where the catcalls and yelling constantly drown out the speaker – it's pandemonium half the time. One of our local village lads will be in the convoy so there's quite a bit of apprehension.*

Talk in the Fuaran is all about 'the Argies,' and the colossal cheek of Argentina to take on the British Empire over the Falkland Islands. I know, it's no longer the British Empire, but most here still think of it that way.

It has all the makings of a comic opera war – started as a distraction from political problems in a faraway land, by a gang of admirals and generals strutting about with big epaulets and gold braid on their uniforms. The Argentine junta is making fierce pronouncements and sending troops off to invade a few small islands in the middle of the South Atlantic, populated mostly by sheep.

Prime Minister Maggie Thatcher has risen to the occasion and sent a fleet of Royal Navy warships and troop transports down that way to boot out the invaders. Argentina thought Britain was bluffing, now the Brits think the Argies are bluffing. No one really believes it will be a shooting war. It all looks like a joke, and in the Fuaran, it is treated as such. More sly comments and snickering than serious war talk. For now, at least.

Donnie Darling is a bit more sober in this regard, anyway – he has a son in the navy whose ship, *HMS Broadsword*, is being dispatched to the war zone. To Donnie and his wife Mary, the Argies may be a joke, but their bullets and bombs could become real enough.

### April 10th

*Last night we went to a dance at the hall – a small crowd, but fun. The band was great – Pete Taylor's bunch – and we danced eightsome reels and strip-the-willow and waltzes until about 2:00 – then went to Jim Muir's for tea and sandwiches.*

*I went with the men a few days ago to get the sheep off Priest Island. I don't know what they thought of my being there – but I had a great time.*

# Priest Island Sheep

The first calm day in early spring is the time to bring the hoggs and gimmers in from the islands. Too young for breeding, the one- and two-year old ewes spend the winter well beyond reach of lusty tups on the mainland. The passing Gulf Stream, having drawn warm Caribbean waters up the eastern shores of North America and across the Atlantic below Greenland, here curls southward along the coast of Britain, keeping the low-lying islands mild through December and January; good grass grows close to the sea even when the hills of Coigach are locked in snow.

We set out on Ian Roll's lovely wooden fishing-cum-tour boat *Hectoria*, the biggest in Old Dornie harbor, with spacious decks well suited for ferrying the sea-bound flock. Ian, Donnie Darling, Kenny Stuart, Ken the Bread, Boysie, Bill Baxter, Barb and I were half the working crew – the other half being a raucous gang of border collies. The dogs seemed to feel they were on holiday, boarding the boat eagerly and pacing the decks like sightseers, peering at porpoises riding the

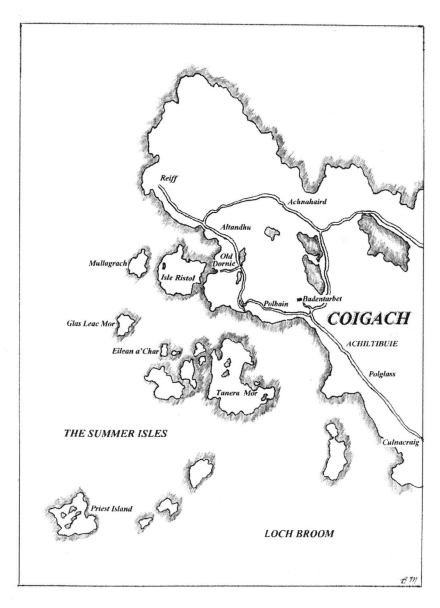

pressure wave ahead of *Hectoria*'s well-rounded bows and exchanging barks with seals basking on sun-warmed rocks at the fringes of the passing islands. The sea was sun-bright and polished for the occasion, disturbed only by the boat's wide-spreading wake, distorting reflections of white-capped Dundonnell mountains across Loch Broom.

Our first port of call was Eilean a' Chléirich, Priest Island, least accessible of the Summer Isles. Once home to an early Christian monastic community, the remote island is uninhabited now and closed to tourists. But local crofters, whose grazing rights predate its establishment as a national bird sanctuary, still winter sheep there.

The landing on Priest was narrow, steep and rocky. A mild swell rose and fell like the breast of a breathing sea, washing the rocks black on the island's rim. *Hectoria* anchored offshore and we untied the large wooden dinghy she'd been towing and rowed into the shadowed cove. Men and dogs scrambled up steep barnacle-covered rocks to reach the greensward above. Priest is about a mile long and equally wide, with a grassy valley running down the center between hills. We split up into two teams to gather sheep from the hills and drive them down the valley to the landing.

Being new to the game, I decided to take my cues from Donnie Darling as we worked in line abreast behind the dogs, pushing the sheep ahead of us. "Come by, Jack, come by," he growled. Obediently I started moving to my left, closing the gap between us.

"Way to me, Jack!" Way? Does he mean 'away' to him, or 'away' from him? I moved back to my right. "Dammit, Jack, get out!" he cried. Thoroughly confused now, I backed off even farther – but again he snarled "Way to me, boy!" Much chagrined, I closed the gap between us again. Walking a straight line on the rough ground was difficult enough – this zigzagging to Donnie's commands was wearing me down.

"Dammit Jack, get off that bitch!" What?!

Then I noticed. The border collie ahead of Donnie had quit working sheep and was enthusiastically humping another dog. The collie's name, of course, was Jack. And my eager attempts to comply with Donnie's orders were simply wasted. "Way to me," "come by," "get out," etc., are traditional sheep dog commands.

The sheep were quite wild after wintering on the island, but once the other Jack got back to business we cornered them all at the head of the rocky cove. Men and dogs forced them down to where young Baxter stood on a ledge and handed them down to Ian Roll, who packed them solid into the waiting dinghy. The two men rowed the dinghy out to *Hectoria* and hoisted them one by one over the rail, then came back for another load. There were about 50 sheep altogether, and it took three trips in the dinghy. Crowding down the steep narrow cove, one of the sheep died; who knew from what – suffocation, injury, fright? Because she didn't belong to any of the men there, her carcass was left on the rocks where the next tide would carry her away.

We picked up a few more sheep from Bottle Island, then unloaded them all at Badenscallie and dropped anchor at Old Dornie late in the day. The whole gang went off to the Fuaran for more than a few pints and drams, where I came to know Bill Baxter, a new face after the closed social life of Coigach winter. Bill's family owns the white house on the hill overlooking Old Dornie harbor.

A cheerful and energetic young man fresh from university, Baxter grew up in Coigach and Tanera and on Scotland's north coast, and moves easily between the big outside world and our small Highland enclave. He regaled us with his adventures as a volunteer in the Sudan and crossing the Sahara in a Land Rover. A willing worker, Bill is a friend of Ian Roll's and well liked in Coigach.

Outside the pub in gathering darkness, the hard-worked dogs waited patiently in their owners' cars. I suspect the one named Jack still had a grin on his face.

Working dogs play a vital role in Coigach, but little sentiment is wasted on them. They are simply tools of the crofter's trade. Donnie kept his border collie locked in a barn, along with a couple of tough little terriers skilled at digging into a fox's den and killing the kits. When one of the terriers dropped a litter, Donnie cast about for willing takers – but there were none. A few days later I asked him how the puppies were doing. "Och," he said with a dismissive wave, "I sent them all off to Stornoway."

Stornoway? That's a port town on the Isle of Lewis, 30 miles off our shore. Why would Donnie send the puppies to Stornoway? Mystified, I later asked Jim Muir. "Oh, that's just Donnie's way of saying they went west with the outgoing tide. In a weighted burlap sack." Oh.

Alasdair West's dogs live in the shell of an old rusty car in the field behind his house. They are good workers, quick to gather in sheep from the hill, responding instantly to his whistled commands. Except for Queenie. She is a bearded collie, with a beautiful long, gray coat, black button eyes and a comical Muppet-like face. Queenie is superb at working sheep close in, holding them tight to a drystone dike and forcing them through narrow gates into the fank. But out on the hill, she is a menace.

The playful beardie loves to rocket through a knot of sheep, scattering them like feathers from a burst pillow. Try as he might, with whistles, commands and curses, Alasdair hasn't managed to break her of this habit. So he usually leaves her back when we are gathering – but sometimes she escapes..

One day, we were working across the hills moving sheep toward the road, the other dogs zigzagging efficiently behind the flock and keeping them in a tight bunch. Queenie suddenly materialized at the crest of a hill and fixed a dark eye on the target below. Even from a distance, you could see her grinning. Alasdair whistled and shouted, but it was too late. The beardie was a gray blur as she shot down the slope and smote the gathered ewes. In one terrible moment, all our labors of the last few hours went for naught as the sheep raced around us and broke for the hills behind.

Queenie was having a wonderful time chasing them. The border collies simply stared in disbelief at the renegade. Alasdair stood silently, arms folded, saying nothing. Eventually the grassy bowl below us was emptied of sheep. Mission accomplished, Queenie came cheerfully trotting back to her master.

"Come here, lass." A quiet but firm command. She sat neatly in front of him, the gray fuzzy face looking up at her master for approval. Alasdair bent down and thrust his crook between the dog's collar and her neck, pushing the long stick deep, deep into the earth. Queenie was skewered to the soft boggy ground. "That should hold you," he muttered. Then he whistled up the border collies and we turned back to gather all over again.

That same day I learned a memorable lesson. We finally got the sheep together again and moving nicely along the road into Achnahaird. Suddenly half a dozen ewes broke away to the right, across a wide open field, racing to get behind us. I ran as fast as I could, stumbling across the grass, mud and rocks in a vain attempt to head them off. Just as the leader was about to get around me, the border collies shot past and turned them back with no apparent effort.

I was soaked in sweat when I got back to the road, my lungs burning and my legs wobbly from the unaccustomed effort. Alasdair came over to where I struggled to catch my breath. He looked up at me through bushy eyebrows and placed a solid, fatherly hand on my heaving shoulder. "Boy," he said, "dogs run. Men walk."

# The Counting of the Yows

Whenever I see a cartoon about someone trying to sleep by counting sheep, I think about the Counting of the Yows in Coigach, an event which has given more than a few crofters sleepless nights of late!

The government pays each West Highland crofter an annual hill sheep subsidy based on the number of breeding ewes – locally "yows" – in his flock. For years, this subsidy has been paid on an honor system, according to the crofters' own tallies. And despite the high standards of education in Highland schools, the sheep men of Coigach have become remarkably inexact about their mathematics.

Folks were thunderstruck, then, when the Scottish Department of Agriculture announced that each flock was to be counted in person by an official inspector! Worse, Her Majesty's Government declared that crofters who couldn't account for ewes they had claimed the previous year would be penalized for earlier subsidies as well.

The Fuaran rumbled with private concern and public indignation.

"Tis a sad thing when a government won't trust its own people," sighed Donnie Darling, whose counting was especially suspect. "Thon heartless Department men have no care at all for how easy it is to lose a yow in these hills."

"Aye," growled the Captain, "and they'll spot one wrong lug mark in a hundred, the baastaards." Lug marks are a distinctive pattern of notches cut in a sheep's ear to prevent one man's ewe from being mistaken for another's. Unfortunately, lug marks also prevented a crofter from padding his official count with ewes 'borrowed' from a cooperative neighbor.

Iain Campbell, who keeps some sheep at Culnacraig with his father John Alec, cheerfully speculated that the man who could invent replaceable sheep ears would do a brisk trade that summer.

In the weeks leading up to The Counting, amazing events were reported up and down the West Coast. Rumors of sheep rustling swept the district; tallies of road kills increased dramatically; men spoke of yows falling into the sea and disappearing without a trace. Alasdair West, who already has one of Coigach's larger flocks, is said to have slipped off quietly to Dingwall market and bought thirty new, unmarked breeding ewes.

Donnie Darling, when a mudslide eroded a hill at the edge of his croft, remarked hopefully, "There's no telling how many yows lie buried under thon mud..." But none of this could erase the signs of worry among the sheep men as the time of The Counting approached.

Donnie had more to worry about than most. He has been tending old Donnie Shaw's 40 ewes along with his own for years, after age and arthritis had bound the ancient bachelor to his wee cottage at the edge of Polbain. Each year, Donnie Shaw and Donnie Darling have filed separate reports to the Department, and been paid separate subsidies, but their ewes have flocked together for so long that only Donnie Darling could pretend to tell them apart.

## April 20th

*This afternoon we went down to visit Joan & Murdo – mostly because we'd learned that Donnie Shaw had died and we wanted to take Murdo's mind off of it. They were good friends and fishing partners in the old days and along with Donnie Darling formed a triumvirate. It's going to be very hard on Donnie – who will he drink with now?*

*Donnie Shaw was to be buried that afternoon so we went down to the church and graveyard with the rest of the community. Murdo claimed yesterday that he couldn't go – but there he was looking pretty good – even took a cord for lowering the coffin (a service always performed by special friends). I was so glad to see him there – I think he'd have felt bad if he hadn't been there to see his friend off.*

Old Donnie Shaw's death came not long before the Counting of the Yows. Among the many folk gathered at the pub after the funeral, Donnie Darling bore his grief most openly, for the older man had been a lifelong friend and neighbor.

"Och, I'll be missing old Donnie," he said sadly, staring pensively into his dram. "That man meant a lot to me."

Just how much he meant became clear some days ago, when the Department inspector finished his tally at Polbain. Donnie Darling's flock, to everyone's surprise, is exactly as claimed in his subsidy application.

And poor old Donnie Shaw, departed now beyond reach of friend and government alike, was a full 40 short.

### April 22nd

*Wilf found a ewe of Donnie Shaw's that was unable to walk. He took her home and fed her whisky and oatmeal (atholl brose). He feeds all his invalid sheep whisky. Jack is threatening to lie in a ditch with his feet in the air so that he can be rescued by Wilf.*

*Sickness and injury seem to be common among the sheep here. The other day Donnie Darling managed to get Jack involved in a rescue effort.*

# Peg-Leg

It was Saturday afternoon, and Donnie was holding forth at the Fuaran when I came in. "Jack, you're a friend of Murdo's aren't you?" I concurred. "I want you to tell him one of his sheep's been hard hit by a car down at Badentarbat."

I questioned him – when did this happen? Where exactly is the sheep? Donnie apparently saw the sheep the preceding evening but had not told anyone about it. Now, being occupied with other matters, he was dropping the problem in my lap.

Returning home, I took Barb and drove down to Badentarbat, scanning the ditches for some sign of the sheep. Finally, while driving back up the road, Barb spotted one lying a short distance up the hillside with her hind legs oddly splayed behind her. I parked the car and walked up. The yow watched me approach until I was within a few feet of her, then began struggling with her front legs. Unable to stand, she rolled over downhill and lay still again.

I had brought a knife in the car, in case the sheep was definitely dying and had to be killed. But I didn't know enough to make that decision myself, so I went back to Murdo's and told him what I'd found.

"Och, it's those people coming from the Fuaran that did it! I never lost a sheep until the Fuaran was there." In Murdo's view, change and bad luck are likely to be connected. Wilf arrived – I had phoned for his help – and we set out together to look at the yow again.

Leaving the Mini at the roadside, we walked up to the sheep. Gently, Wilf knelt down beside her and, while I held her head, he probed and flexed her back legs. "Nothing broken here, no, nothing broken at all." One leg was quite stiff, and he worked it until it moved freely again. "I don't think she's been injured at all," he said. "I think it's that swayback paralysis. Let's get her back to Murdo's and put her in the barn."

Putting my hands under her forelegs, I lifted the yow – she was heavy in lamb – and carried her down the hill, her wet wool soaking through my pants legs. I laid her at the side of the road to wait while Wilf drove the Mini back and fetched his Renault, which was big enough to carry her. While waiting, I stroked the yow's head and talked to her, trying to keep her calm. She tried at first to get up again, but then resigned herself to this peculiar fate and lay quietly under my hand.

In a few minutes Wilf returned. We loaded the yow into the back of his car and drove up the road and into Murdo's drive. Wilf took her hind legs, I took her forelegs and together we carried her back through the muck to the barn, where we put her down on clean dry straw. Wilf brought her an armload of hay, and gently forced a handful of dry clover into her month. She chewed it loudly. We left her there, still eating, and walked back to Murdo's house. The vet was coming to Coigach in a few days, and would decide what to do with the crippled yow.

On Thursday afternoon I stopped by to have tea with Murdo and Joan. Gale force winds and hail beat at the window, and bitter cold made the coal fire all the more welcoming in the little house. About 4 o'clock there came a knock at the door – Ian Muir, the young vet, was making his fortnightly calls around Coigach. A good-looking chap in his twenties, he grew up in Polbain. Although his veterinary practice is based on the east coast in Dingwall, he still comes back to Coigach regularly to serve the needs of the community – taking care of everything from cows at the hotel to cats and dogs, pet sheep and hill sheep.

Joan, Ian and I went out to the shed on the back end of the barn. Snow blew through gaps in the walls, hail beat against the corrugated iron roof. Two sheep lay in the shed: the cripple, which Wilf had named Peg-Leg, and an older yow which had been down with pneumonia. Ian tended the old one first, checking her temperature and respiration. "She's over the pneumonia, but I doubt her lungs will ever recover." He gave her an injection, then turned his attention to Peg-Leg.

The vet pulled the yow to her feet – she struggled with her front legs as before; but the back legs were still. When he supported her back end, Peg-Leg began kicking, and stamping with one back leg – a sign of progress! Ian probed, poked, flexed the legs, then let her down again. "I think she'll be alright. There's something in her spine that's causing this. It might be an injury, or an abscess – but – she seems to be improving." He recommended giving her support every day to help her flex and re-learn to use her legs.

Ian also told Joan to take up a piece of corrugated iron sheeting on the floor, which she had put there to cover a wet spot. "If your Peg-Leg tries to walk and slips on that, she'll lose confidence and give up. She'll need good solid footing under her if she's to walk again." Whether in fact Peg-Leg does so is a question, to be answered another day.

## April 28th

*The first cuckoo of spring!! Hoorah! Jack went with the Manager to look for foxes. They hunt them now because of the lambs coming. I'm glad they didn't find any – although the foxes do kill lambs and I can see why they have to get rid of them.*

*The new lambs are starting to appear. The first one came two days ago. The weather has been squally with some cold rain – rather worrisome with the new lambs coming. Lambing is going well so far – we haven't had the traditional lambing snow and we're all holding our breath. The shepherds are all tired from continually walking the hills – there's been lots of twins and big lambs, due to the early winter being so mild – but that means more work for the shepherds because deliveries are harder and because they try to foster twins off (a ewe has a hard time feeding two on the scant feed they get here).*

# Peg-Leg's Lamb

This morning Peg-Leg had her lamb, but it was born dead. Murdo hobbled out to the shed and carefully removed the skin from the little carcass. He trimmed it into the shape of a vest and fitted it onto an orphan lamb, which he presented to the yow's muzzle. Peg-Leg eagerly nuzzled the orphan's familiar-smelling little fleece. When Murdo set the lamb down by her side, the little one promptly tucked its head under and butted her swollen udder, letting down the life-giving milk. Peg-Leg seemed quite content.

With sheep wandering about Coigach in large numbers, injuries happen and so do deaths, and you'd think one more yow or lamb wouldn't make much difference. But they do. And for an old man who had all but given up on his own life, success at fostering the lamb gave a bit of a lift as well.

# War

## April 29th

*Joanie said the other day "someone at the store was asking if you were going to buy Castlehill." We said "we'd love to if we were rich" – which is the truth. I really don't know if they want to sell – and I certainly don't know what our plans are. Anyway – it was a surprise – and most interesting.*

*The Falklands thing is heating up. If it gets to an all-out shooting war and things go badly (lots of casualties), Maggie Thatcher could be in trouble. The whole thing is so stupid! I don't think Britain could do anything but what she's doing at this point – but the whole thing should have been negotiated a long time ago. Well – they're in it now. It'll be interesting to see what happens.*

# Fitting In

One of my favorite artists is Alexander Calder, whose mobiles grace every major art museum in the world. And Coigach society is much like one of Calder's mobiles – a cosmic collection of human clusters, all moving gently around each other, connected yet separate, different in many ways, yet interdependent – and all hanging from the thread of a single track road.

Each individual cluster of people orbits around a common theme; the gravitational pull of social class, education, religion, or birthplace binds them together. Yet in the ever-changing dynamic of community, individuals from different clusters are constantly drifting close enough to touch and affect each other every day.

These social clusters aren't rigid or exclusive – you can't afford to be exclusive in Coigach, where everyone depends on everyone else. So people from all walks of life work and live side by side here, meet in the shops, chat in the pubs, and freely exchange friendships and favors. Yet everyone knows precisely where everyone else fits in.

At the outer edges of this social mobile are the "white settlers"- people who live elsewhere most of the year, but own property in Coigach which they use for summer holidays. Among these seasonal residents are sub-clusters defined by age, class, wealth and education. Some "white settlers" are satisfied to pass across the surface of the community; others nurture strong friendships with local families, 'muck in' when there's work to be done, and become valued if ephemeral residents.

Closer in are the "incomers" – people who have come in from the outside and settled into the community. Many are working people who contribute to the local economy. The new arrivals may be accepted by some locals, resented by others; it makes no difference, they are here to stay. Many have families, and children in the Achiltibuie school who will someday become "locals" themselves.

Among the incomers are pensioners from elsewhere in the UK who have chosen, inexplicably, to spend their golden years fighting rain, wind, cold, mildew and isolation. The up side is that they're unlikely to be burgled, robbed or beaten here, and they can rest their eyes on some of the most serene and glorious land- and seascapes on earth. If it isn't raining.

At the center of this little cosmos are the "locals" – people born here, families whose connections to the land and sea go back generations. They have a deep rooted sense of belonging, know the old place names and stories and sing the old songs their ancestors knew. And even though they may no longer be a majority in their own place, they're proud to carry the cultural DNA that defines the character of Coigach. Being "local" is an aristocratic title to which many aspire, but which only birth can confer.

Wafting gently though this social mobile, causing motion without real change, are the tourists – locally called, for unknown reasons, "bonglies." They appear with the sun every year, graciously contribute to the local economy, and drift away after a week or two. Bonglies populate the beach campsite at Achnahaird, the youth hostel, the Summer Isles Hotel, and holiday chalets and B&Bs all around the Coigach coast. They tour the islands on *Hectoria*. They trudge through the rain in blue- and yellow-slickered lines to the top of Stac Pollaidh. They crowd the lounge bar in the Fuaran and monopolize the tiny pool table. And then they disappear, and no one remembers their names.

Into this balanced cosmos we've come like weightless birds, able to flit from group to group because we carry none of the burdens of British class-consciousness. Our mangled English defies the UK habit of assuming status by accent. As Barb says, we have no class whatsoever. In our middle years, we're at ease with old and young alike. In life experience, we're familiar with both hardship and privilege. In some ways, we have more social freedom than most who live here.

What keeps people apart here isn't antipathy or snobbishness (though none of us is immune to them). It's just that, as in every other society, people tend to associate with people like themselves. And just as we quickly note any ties that bind us together, we can never completely ignore our differences, or forget where we belong.

This all came to mind a few weeks after Donnie Shaw's funeral. Standing at the bar in the Summer Isles, Donnie Darling was again mulling over the vagaries of fate and the mortality of man. "Old Donnie Shaw's passing," he sighed, "leaves me the last of the local crofters in Polbain."

"But Donnie," I asked, "what about Murdo?"

"Murdo?!" He snorted. "Murdo belongs to Tanera!"

## May 2nd

*Lost three lambs in the last two days. The weather is terrible – cold with driving wind and hail like shrapnel. Donnie says that if it keeps up we won't have a lamb alive at week's end. I think we're in for a bad spring and summer.*

*The grazing here is poor and ewes don't have enough milk to successfully raise twins, so they take one off and foster it onto a ewe who's lost her own lamb. W&W have a little one now that's to be fostered onto a ewe in the morning. Her lamb (Murdo's – the first one born in the village) fell into a burn and drowned, poor little thing.*

*There is shooting now in the Falklands – Argentina is making wild claims of victory – it's unbelievable how they can lie so blatantly. It's a shame to see it come to war status.*

# Pet Sheep

West Highlanders who work with sheep will tell you it's no good making pets of them. "Once they're spoiled like that, you can never work them with hill sheep," they'll say. "Pet sheep don't respect man or dog." Odds are good that the speaker knows from first hand experience, having a spoiled pet sheep or two of his own in the steading behind his house.

Pet sheep usually achieve this privileged rank by being runt or orphan lambs needing bottle feeding, though sometimes mature ewes swindle their way into the steading through sickness or injury.

However they get there, once a sheep has been gently tended and nurtured, round the clock, by the crofter or his wife, it tends to become part of the household menagerie.

In recent times, some of the incomers to Coigach, retired folk and such, have taken to raising orphaned lambs as pets. At first, local crofters welcomed this; they thought giving the wee ones away would relieve them of a perennial nuisance during the hectic days of the lambing. But many have thought again, since Donnie Darling had his heart problem, which he claims was brought on by Wilf Bell and his pet sheep.

When the Bells came up from England some years ago, Wilf threw his considerable intelligence and boundless energy into learning the ways of his new Highland home. Wilf is one of those confident men who know almost all there is to know, and believe they can learn the rest of it in a day.

After he adopted his first pet sheep, a wether, or castrated male, he called 'Fred', Wilf began to follow Donnie Darling on his rounds, asking a thousand questions. Donnie, like every other crofter in Coigach, fancies himself the best source of genuine sheep wisdom in the West Highlands. Naturally, he was pleased that this English fellow recognized his genius. And for a while, Wilf and Donnie were inseparable.

But it wasn't long before Wilf's questions about sheep became comments. Then his comments became theories. Soon his theories grew critical of local hill sheep raising practices in general, and Donnie's in particular. Thereafter came a parting of the ways for Wilf and Donnie.

Undaunted, Wilf set out to prove his theories on an accumulation of pet sheep, each with its own name: Fred, Frieda, Minnie, Flora, Ealasaid, and Barabel. No children of royal blood have better care than Wilf Bell's sheep. They are hand fed, stuffed with vitamin supplements, pumped full of the latest miracle drugs, sheltered from wind and rain, bedded on fresh hay.

Wilf and Wendy are devoted to their pets, moving them daily to get better grazing, or sometimes, as they say "just to keep the sheep from getting bored." And the sheep have responded by growing fat and woolly and twice the size of the crofters' ewes on the hills above Achiltibuie. This alone would have irritated Donnie, even if Wilf hadn't blathered a bit about his lovely sheep and intimated his superior skill as a stockman. The lifelong crofter argued that there was some difference between hand raising six pets and managing a large flock of hill sheep, but Wilf always knew better.

"Sheep are sheep, Donnie," he'd say with a knowing smile.

Despite having been castrated, Freddy the wether is undisputed king of Bell's miniature flock. The ewes were never bred, but kept segregated and celibate during the breeding time – giving rise to jokes around Coigach about "virgin wool." But the Bells are adamant about keeping their ewes innocent. "It wouldn't be fair to poor Freddy," Wendy would whisper. "He's not able, you know."

Of course, Wilf's pampered pets never mix on the common grazing with Donnie's wild-eyed, scrawny hill sheep, which forage on heather, gorse and sparse grasses across the slopes above the village. But the Bells' sheep can't avoid the ordinary flock at dipping time. By law, all sheep have to be dipped in a chemical bath at prescribed times of the year, to prevent the spread of disease. It's a community activity, requiring plenty of water, chemicals, and man and dog power to handle the struggling beasts.

On the day in question, Donnie had spent long hours gathering his wild, evasive flock stumping over miles of rough ground, stumbling through bog and burn, waving his stick, sweating and shouting and swearing at his dogs to bring his ewes down toward the old Polbain fank with its pens funneling in to the dipper. Short of breath and red of face, he stopped for a moment to roll a cigarette and watch his neighbors' flocks gather in.

Wilf, of course, brought his sheep galloping up from the crofts in a minute, simply by calling Freddy's name and rattling an oat bucket.

Bell's well fed pets mixed in with the scraggy hill sheep, looking like six fat marshmallows in a pan of white peas. A dozen crofters and their dogs formed a line, working the mass of baaing, reluctant animals down the field. Here and there a few ewes tried to bolt away, but alert border collies cut them off and forced them back toward the waiting fank.

Everything went well for Donnie and his friends until that critical moment when the sheep had been driven against the fank wall. The beasts could smell the noxious chemicals awaiting them; they didn't want to enter the open gate. Frozen in fear and suspicion, they scanned the line of men and dogs who'd trapped them, looking for a chance to break through.

The men were tense, trying to contain the anxious flock until a sheep or two might trickle through the gate into the fank. Once that happened, the others would follow – like sheep. But until that first hoped for entry, one wrong move could panic the whole flock into explosive escape.

It was at this moment of suspended animation and breathless anxiety that Wilf, standing behind the line of shepherds, caught the eye of his best beloved pet in the midst of the hill sheep. Almost as a reflex he raised his hand, waved, and cooed: "Hellooo, Freddy!"

A woolly head shot up from the flock. The huge beast bolted joyfully toward his master. Two hundred hill sheep followed, dodging dogs and bowling men over, rushing headlong toward the wild high ground and freedom. Within minutes the last of them had scattered into the hills. The only sheep left in sight were six fat white pets, crowding eagerly around an embarrassed Wilf Bell and nuzzling his oat bucket.

It was that same afternoon Donnie was taken off to hospital at Inverness with a heart problem.

# War

Jubilation in the pub – submarine *HMS Conqueror* torpedoed an Argentine cruiser. Laughter, toasts, predictions of a quick and easy victory. From the enthusiasm of my neighbors, it could be a World Cup match rather than a shooting war. But over 300 Argentine sailors went down with the *Belgrano*, and now the junta is rejecting all peace proposals. Looks like they're digging in for a fight.

## May 4th

*Argentine aircraft using French Exocet missiles sink the British destroyer* HMS Sheffield *with twenty men killed. One British Harrier plane is shot down. The grim reality of war is sinking in, and everyone is now concerned about young Donnie.*

## May 12th

*The weather is holding. We've been out walking the lambing parks – helped Alasdair bring in a ewe with a dead lamb to get a foster lamb – and today down at Dornie with Donnie we helped pen and birth a ewe who'd been trying since early morning to lamb. I held her head while Donnie delivered the lamb. The baby had a tough time and took a while getting to his feet. We left the mother licking it over, and went back to the field where there's a lamb whose mother has no milk and it has to be fed 2-3 times a day by bottle. He's a bit on the shaky side – but comes running when he sees Donnie.*

## A Tradition Begins

### May 18th

*Wonder of wonders – we got a phone call from Murdo today asking if Jack wanted to take him to the pub. He hasn't been for a year or more – since his stroke – and has often said "Those days are over – I'll never go there again." Pretty chipper he's been since the good weather's come. In fact I've seen improvement for some time now, but he'd never admit it.*

On Saturday I picked up Murdo at his house about midday – a time I was pretty sure there would be a few old friends at the Fuaran he'd know. Although the day was mild, Joan had him swaddled in jacket, scarf, hat and a long woolen overcoat, and fluttered about as if we were bound for the Arctic. She was pleased he was going, yet concerned about this, his first venture to the pub since his stroke. "Now mind, don't you be late coming back for tea!" As we drove up the road toward Altandhu, I could see her in the rearview mirror, standing by the gate watching until we disappeared from sight.

Parking the Mini close to the Fuaran's door, I helped extract the large man from the small car. Leaning on my arm just a little, Murdo shuffled into the pub. It was almost empty, but Alasdair and John Alec Campbell were standing at the bar as we came in. Their faces lit up at seeing the old man.

At the end of the bar was Big Leslie, a cheerful buxom redhead with a ribald sense of humor. "Well, Murdo. And how have you been?"

The old man sighed. "Up and down," he moaned. "Up and down."

She laughed. "Ha! You should be so lucky!"

The other men chuckled, but I don't think the old bachelor got it. I helped him to a seat by the bar, and before I could reach for my wallet, John Alec had his money out and Andy was passing a round of drinks across. The three old friends were soon at it, exchanging Coigach's conversational currency of weather and fishing, sheep and people.

John Alec is in his 70s, a vigorous old man with broad shoulders and a strong jaw that could have been drawn with a T-square. He is a widower, born in Polglass and living in Culnacraig where his wife grew up. It is the last house on the paved road beyond Achiltibuie, where it comes to an end on the flanks of Ben More Coigach.

In earlier times John Alec had worked as a ghillie, or guide, for sportsmen coming up from England for the fishing or shooting. In Gaelic, 'ghillie' means 'boy,' although it's a job for a man, and an experienced one at that. Now he is more or less retired from ghillying, but still goes up on the hill to tend his sheep. He is sharp of wit and tongue, and loves to get people arguing so he can step aside and laugh.

Alasdair is the youngest of the three, still working on the road gang and keeping about 300 sheep at Achnahaird. His wife Margaret is Donnie Darling's sister, so his sons and daughters, like John Alec's, are doubly 'local' – a distinction few in Coigach can claim.

Donnie Darling came in and joined us, adding his own fount of stories to the mix. These are men who had grown up in a world far different from yours and mine. They had passed their youth in what author William Manchester called "a world lit only by fire," reaching adulthood before electricity came to Coigach. Now they are living bridges between a traditional life little changed for centuries, and an era of restless technology and social disruption. They know that their time is passing, and they accept it with good grace without forgetting the value of what's being left behind.

I could follow most of their conversation, except when one or the other occasionally lapsed into Gaelic when no English word would do. Their talk was comfortable and quiet, and flowed from the now into the past, to times they'd had, adventures shared and companions kept in memory. Whenever a new name was mentioned, the story would pause until everyone was satisfied he knew exactly which Hector or Duncan or Ian was meant.

Murdo and Alasdair recounted a youthful ploy when they tried to catch sea trout by moonlight from the Garvie. They suspended baited hooks from a wooden board that had a long line extending from each end. The would-be poachers waded into the water and manipulated the hand lines, trying to float the angled board out into deeper currents where the fish might be feeding. As it turned out, the boys caught little more than chills from standing neck deep in the cold dark river. But the old men could still chuckle at the memory.

The give and take of their conversation was largely alien to me and I was more spectator than participant. Yet they never made me feel excluded. Just being among men like these is a joy and a privilege, and I was content to hold my tongue and listen. The atmosphere of companionship was all-encompassing. And gently warmed, of course, by a dram or two. Or three.

Afterward, Murdo and I went back to his house. Barb had walked down from Castlehill, and Joan was bustling about, preparing little plates of biscuits or pancakes or crackers with cheese to go with copious doses of milky tea. We sat by the fire and talked of the day's events, who was at the pub and who was not and who said what about whom. Wilf stopped in to brighten the room with silly jokes and news of his pet sheep and tales of his days in the RAF during World War II.

When Joan set a plate by his chair, Murdo retrieved his store-bought teeth from the pocket of his wooly cardigan. Popping them into his mouth, he began to tell stories.

We mentioned visiting Sandwood Bay when we were here last and he said "Oh you know there's a ghost connected with Sandwood Bay" and then told us that there had been a shipwreck there and the bodies had washed up on the beach. Among them was the ship's captain, whose fingers were covered with gold rings. After the bodies had been buried a local fellow had dug up the captain and taken his rings – so now he walks the night looking for his gold. Murdo said that when he was in hospital the man next to him was an old shepherd in that area, and one night he'd gone down to the beach and stayed in the hut so he could gather his sheep in the morning. He said that all of a sudden during the night his dogs began to howl and tremble and he couldn't quiet them. He spent a most uncomfortable night.

Murdo and Joan both said that there was definitely a ghost on Tanera. A man who owned the house near the old cannery was much troubled by the ghost, who kept him from sleeping and moved things about etc., so he sent for a person who was known to be able to get rid of ghosts. The person said that yes, he could exorcise the ghost, but the man would pay dearly for it in personal loss. The man still was desperate to rid himself of the ghost and said to go ahead. Soon after that the man's two sons died and his crops all failed. A price indeed!

Since that first outing, these early Saturday afternoons at the Fuaran have become a regular thing. We can almost always count on John Alec and Alasdair to be there, and they and Murdo have become known in the pub as "The Worthies." Some other folk are coming out at the same time now, just knowing there'll be good crack about old times. Everyone seems pleased that Murdo is back in circulation, however limited, after he had all but disappeared from community life.

Of course, going back afterward for tea with Joan and Barb has become an established tradition, too.

## May 21st

*All efforts to solve the Falkland dispute by diplomacy have now fallen through, so it's expected that Britain will invade the islands in the next few days. In fact they've already gone in with raiding parties. Donnie Darling is worried about young Donnie – they got a letter yesterday, but it was three weeks getting here. They don't know where the Broadsword is at the moment – whether it's involved with the latest hostilities or not.*

*Meanwhile, the Pope, who is due to visit Britain in a week's time, is vacillating about coming. When his visit was announced months ago, there was much controversy, especially in Scotland. I have experienced bigotry for the first time. There is lots of anti-Catholic feeling here, though most people are polite enough not to voice it. But there is one old man from the council houses who has been very abusive (hates Americans, Irish and especially Catholics). It's been an interesting experience.*

*Jim Muir brought us some mackerel for supper – I'll fix them with mustard sauce. Jim has given Jack several books now to read – one is a collection of verse by William McGonagall – the worst poet Scotland has ever produced – but prolific! The other is a book on boats and fishermen and looks fascinating.*

*We've met a whole group of new people that we've really enjoyed. Bill Baxter owns the house above Dornie Harbor. He's doing construction work on it this summer so is here with a friend for a few months. We were invited up to the house for dinner and had a thoroughly enjoyable evening there.*

*The Worthies: Murdo, John Alec and Alasdair West at the Fuaran*

*Spring: Taking young sheep off Priest Island*

*Autumn: dipping at Badentarbat*

*Summer morning: Wendy Stewart plays at Castlehill*

# Improvers

There has never been a shortage of suggestions for improving the Highlands, and the inhabitants thereof. Wealthy landowners in the 19th century tried to improve the area by clearing off the people and replacing them with sheep. Rich industrialists experimented with model villages and model factories here and there, or extravagant gardens planted with exotic species. Academics bought offshore islands in hope of turning them into agricultural Edens. It is almost reflexive for visitors and even incomers to think up ways to make these remote lands more productive – "if only the locals would just (your suggestion here)."

I know one retired fellow here, from Orkney, who insists that an influx of hard-working Orcadians would make poor barren Coigach bloom like their rich green homeland. Another from the Lowlands avers that a better breed of sheep would do the trick, along with modern scientific animal husbandry. Several from England just know that a more industrious race would prosper here. Outsiders generally seem to think the Highlands are wasted on the Highlanders, that generations of isolation, ignorance and indolence have reduced the area to poverty, and that fresh ideas are the answer to everything. After all, how could such spectacularly beautiful country be so unproductive?

If they'd try to turn a shovel of dirt on a croft, they'd have their answer. Coigach is poor land, more rock and acid peat than arable soil. The miles of drystone dikes that delineate crofts and roads and march up hills were built with the labor of generations, as much to stow the stones somewhere as to create barriers. Atlantic storms build speed and strength across 3,000 miles of open ocean until they strike the Northwest Highlands and hammer into submission any living thing that tries to grow. Deep beds of peat provide some warmth in the cutting, more in the hauling and stacking by the door, most in glowing on the hearth – but no energy for growing anything other than heather and gorse, and damn little nutrient for sheep of any breed.

In short, it's a testament to human perseverance that any people have managed to survive here at all, much less build the vibrant Gaelic culture renowned for wit and music and gracious hospitality. So, rather than go on about how the local folk in Coigach could do better, I wanted to learn how they did as well as they did. And for instruction, I fixed on one man who I felt was exemplary.

We've made many good friends in Coigach, friends across the social spectrum, locals and incomers, laborers and professionals, youngsters and pensioners. And many a story I could tell about them all. But the people who have taken the strongest hold on me are the ones whose time is passing. Who spoke Gaelic at their mothers' knees, grew up in houses lit by lamps and warmed by peat, and recall the day electricity first came to Coigach. Who have the Highlands in their blood and hold to Highland ways, even as they bend under the onslaught of tourism, television, and the invasion of strangers like myself.

Alasdair West is one of those rare men who seldom entertains doubts about himself or the world he lives in. Each day he can step from the door of his house and look at the same hills and fields, the same sweep of beach, the same sea his father and grandfather knew, and all who came before them. A stocky man who always wears his cap at a jaunty angle, he walks and speaks with confidence, and what he says is usually worth listening to.

Alasdair still cuts peats with the help of his sons, and keeps a good stack of them inside the gate by his house. It isn't that he's old-fashioned – he just knows the value of traditional ways that others have carelessly discarded.

I don't know what he made of me at first – this pushy American fellow who pestered him at the pub, haunted his fank, and apparently thought the weather could be made to follow a timetable. I think he was puzzled, perhaps a bit bothered, but also amused – and too kind to push me away. To my constant eager questions he gives patient replies, often rubbing a flake of black tobacco between calloused hands, packing his pipe and taking a puff before answering. There is little small talk in him, but quiet humor and honest warmth and strong opinions.

Sharp eyes and sharper tongues cut through a small community like Coigach. If you want to know a man's flaws, just ask his neighbor. To be fair, gossip here is more for sport than spite. In these verbal duels, touches are scored but blood is seldom drawn, and no one is beyond comment and criticism. Yet in the time we've been here, I've never heard a word against Alasdair West – he's that kind of man.

## May 25th

*I am down with a miserable cold at the moment – Jack has had one for weeks. Everyone in the whole community either has it or is recovering from the same bug. At the moment I can't talk – just whisper. I even cough in a whisper.*

*Yesterday we stopped in to see Donnie & Mary's new house (they're finally all moved in). It's really nice – with great views from all the windows. We stayed for tea and really enjoyed the visit.*

*Things are greening up now. The new bracken is uncurling and a haze of green is appearing on the winter brown hills. We've had a little rain and it brings a new rush of growth. Everything looks new and bright – especially with the gorse at full bloom along the roads. The rhododendrons are coming into bloom near Ullapool and make a splashy show of color.*

## May 27th

*Today I've felt much better and could go out and do some yard work. Jack cut the lawn with an old scythe he found in the steading. The smell of the new cut grass, along with the rowans' blossoming, was sweet indeed. The weather has been windy and showery for the past week but I've been too sick to go out anyway.*

*The Pope finally decided to come tomorrow. It should be an interesting visit.*

*We heard today that HMS Broadsword received some damage but it wasn't too bad. Donnie and Mary are spending some sleepless nights – every time there's an engagement they have to call a central number to get information on casualties. It's hard on them.*

*Days are incredibly long now – it's still light at 11:00 p.m. and you can see light behind Castle Hill after midnight. I'd love to see midsummer's eve here – it's light then all night long.*

# Summer

## Up with the Cuckoos

As spring rolls on toward summer, the sun here moves farther and farther north and the hours of darkness dwindle to less than a handful. The cuckoo birds on the hill start calling around three o'clock in the morning. When they do, I always wake up and look at my wrist.

In our house in America, we had a lovely old German cuckoo clock that reliably struck the quarter hours. On wakeful nights the little wooden birds used to give me comfort, announcing the hour without requiring me to open my eyes. Now the real cuckoos make the exact same sound, and I feel compelled to check my watch, and I have to report that the live birds have a damn poor sense of time.

It isn't all that much of a problem, though. I have always loved early mornings, and do most of my writing work in the quiet time when saner folk are still asleep. This habit allows me to peck away at the typewriter for a few hours without any distractions. Eventually Barb will get up and bring me a cup of tea, and some time thereafter I'll hear her starting breakfast. Often I bring into the kitchen whatever I've just written, and we discuss it over morning coffee. She is my audience, my sounding board, my editor who gently brings me down to earth without bruising my ego.

It's a pleasant routine for a writer – one I have enjoyed for many years. Now she tells me that routine will be interrupted. Barb wants to go back to America to see how the kids are doing. Once a Mom, always a Mom, she can't be satisfied with occasional letters or even phone calls from across the Atlantic. After almost a year of separation, she needs a few weeks of hugs from the girls, hugs from her parents, time to visit with lifelong friends. Then she'll be back replenished, ready for another year at this end of the Wee Mad Road.

I'm planning to stay on here, and look on her impending absence with mixed feelings. It will give me almost a month of solitude in which to concentrate on writing the novel, without the temptations of long lazy tea times and visits and walks together along the shore and over the hills. On the other hand, I am the most married of men and never completely happy without her.

Well, I have until mid-June to get used to the idea, and I should be able to survive three weeks or so on my own. I guess.

## June 6th

*Yesterday was another glorious warm day. We took a picnic up to Inchnadamph for the sheep dog trials, which were held in a beautiful green field on the shore of Loch Assynt. Each dog had to get five sheep and run them through a course of gates – then pen them, after which he had to cut one out of the bunch and keep it out. The shepherd stood at one end of the field and directed the dog by whistles, shouts or hand signals and the dog had to take the sheep around the course, which was quite a long distance.*

*There was a lapwing that had a nest in the field and every time a dog would go out the bird would dive at it and harrass it all the way down the field. Only one dog all day had a perfect run. Most either missed the center gate or couldn't get the sheep penned (they did not want to go in and they're phenomenally sneaky!). But it was a joy to watch the dogs work – they're so eager and enjoy it all. All the dogs are small black and white border collies. The day was hot but there was a nice breeze blowing off the Loch which made it pleasant – still it was warm work for dogs & sheep.*

# The Salmon Fishery

From the tee intersection where the single track meets Loch Broom, take a turn to the right. The road runs flat between a green, where stand the ruins of an old stone fank, and a pretty little beach, before it climbs around the hill and disappears toward Polbain. The beach is called Badentarbat, and it is the center of Coigach's traditional salmon fishery.

Let me make a distinction here. Most of the salmon you buy in supermarkets today have spent their lives as captives. They are hatched in commercial hatcheries, and transferred to huge cages suspended in the sea. They're fed with pellets made from ground up 'trash' fish, sand eels, or whatever form of nutrient is cheapest at the moment. And as they grow their meat is flabby, colorless and unattractive.

Not long before they're harvested from the cages for slaughter, modern salmon farm management dictates a change in diet. Electronic feeding machines drop special pellets into the sea cage, artificially inducing into their flesh the rosy pink you expect your salmon to have. Nothing can be done about the flabby flesh, though, for life in a cage provides little exercise. The result is an affordable piece of salmon-shaped, salmon-colored fish which joins a thousand other manufactured products in your grocery.

Wild salmon, on the other hand, have firm flesh, natural color and superior flavor. But it takes more labor – and luck – to produce a wild salmon. Most of the wild salmon here are caught in large underwater traps called bag nets. It's not really a bag – just an area fenced in by netting, pinned to the ocean floor and rigged to the surface with spars and floats. The bag net has only one entrance – and no exit. A long section of net called a 'leader' heads off the wild fish as they migrate close to shore and channels them toward the entrance into the trap.

When enough salmon have been trapped, they are dipped out of the open-topped traps with long-handled nets, wielded by young men in brightly painted clinker-built wooden boats. The boats are called 'cobles,' and the young men are called 'loons,' and I can't tell you why. Nor can I say how long this small, labor-intensive wild salmon fishery will be able to compete against the corporate sea farms. But the salmon station at Badentarbat, with its whitewashed stone ice house and net shed and fisherman's bothy, has been there for more than a century, and the beached cobles and anchors and great spreads of drying nets are a colorful part of the Coigach scene.

A mile off shore, in the old anchorage of Tanera Mor, float the sea cages of a commercial salmon farm. Here too, young men from the community work in open boats to tend the captive fish. But where the bag-netters bring in salmon by the dozens, the sea-farms measure fish by the tons. The cold clear waters of Loch Broom are ideal for sea farming, and tens of thousands of salmon are grown and harvested here every year.

Loch Broom has a long history of commercial fishing. Herring by the millions – perhaps billions – once swarmed the waters off Scotland. Local men in small, open sailing boats scoured the turbulent sea to harvest the glistening bounty. In the 1780s, the British Fisheries Society built a fish processing factory on Tanera Mor, with a long stone jetty where fishermen could off-load their catches, and large sailing ships could take on barrels of salted herring for the home markets of Holland, Germany and France.

The herring fishery boomed in the 19th century; there were jobs to be had and money to be made as more and more people chased fewer and fewer fish. When herring became few enough, the fishing industry turned to the next best thing. Cod. Haddock. Salmon. One by one, the wild fish of the sea dwindled under the onslaught. What's left today is not enough to fill the cases in the fish markets, so 'sea farming' has become the next best thing.

## June 8th

*On Monday we went to Inverpolly to watch them load salmon smolts (about 8 inches long) from the hatchery tanks into the truck. The water in the tank is lowered, the fish tranquilized with a powdered chemical, netted and transferred into tanks on the truck. Extra oxygen is pumped into the tanks because of the reduced water.*

*At Badentarbat the fish are emptied out through long plastic tubes into the large open holding tank of a Norwegian purser that has been adapted for holding live fish. It is a sharp looking boat – bright orange and spotlessly clean. They were shipping over 90,000 smolts (worth £1 each) to Orkney and Shetland where they'll be held in sea cages until they're fully-grown and ready for market. Calum had the boat take smolts over to Lewis for his own farm there – and all the Norwegian crew were sick. They had to go around the Butt of Lewis and they weren't used to seas like that!*

*Today's a lovely hazy summer day. We went down to Dornie this morning – Jack's been helping Ian Roll varnish the Hectoria.*

*Ian wasn't there so we talked to Ken and Jim for a while until they went off to sea with the salmon nets. Jack spent the afternoon (in fact he's still there) working on the boat. I went over to W&W's and watched the Pope's appearance in Glasgow. Anne Irish and Fr. Brady went down for it, so I had to watch it on TV at least.*

*British troops are attacking Port Stanley in the Falklands – that will be decisive anyway. What then? Who knows?*

## June 10th

*Two beautiful hot days. Yesterday we went fishing with Wilf for most of the day. Not much action in the way of fish, but saw a whole school of porpoise, a pair of gannets, lots of black guillemots, shags, great northern divers and a great group of seals. There was one huge black bull that was most impressive. They were very curious and would stand up quite high in the water and look at us. I spent the evening working in the garden – until the midges came out in clouds about 9:10 p.m. It hardly gets dark now at all.*

*Today we took a picnic and went out on a boat with Bill Baxter and his helper Ian. Bill owns Glas Leac Mor, so we fished until we'd caught a box of cuddies – then went over to the island, built a fire to fry up the fish and ate them with potato salad and other goodies. The day had been hot inland – but out on the sea it was lovely and cool.*

*Sat in the sun and watched the seals as we ate – then walked all around the island. The sea pinks and wild flowers were in bloom and the gulls, shags, fulmars and graylag geese were nesting. We saw a chick hatching from a brown-speckled gull's egg, and a newly hatched shag chick. Its mother squawked at us – her throat and mouth bright yellow inside, her head moving threateningly on her snaky neck.*

*When we started home Bill was gutting fish in the stern – and that brought the gulls to follow. With the red ball of sun behind us and white wings flashing as the birds hovered in changing patterns above the boat, it was one of the most beautiful sights I've ever seen. The islands were in rosy light, with velvety green tops and the cliffs and skerries highlighted by the setting sun.*

*We went up to Bill's after we got back and watched the sun go down over Old Dornie. It was a glowing ball that reflected in the water – the sea and sky being the same color, the bright orange reflection seemed to just hang there. Fantastic. Bill shot a rabbit for us this evening, so we'll have him & Ian over for a meal next week. Later we went to the Summer Isles for a pint and a nice visit with friends there. The Fuaran is full of bonglies right now, it being Whitsun week and an English holiday.*

# Drink

By now you have noticed that we mention whisky frequently, and seem to spend an inordinate amount of time in pubs. My only excuse is that as an exotic species here, we are simply adapting to a different ecosystem. Drinking is almost as natural to the Highlands as breathing, and sometimes – when the air is raw with cold and wind – infinitely more pleasurable. Good manners dictate that you accept a drink that's offered. Good sense dictates that you don't let it go to waste.

Drink is offered here when you come into anyone's house. Drink is passed around when work is finished. Drink is at the center of every ceilidh, every dinner, and – of course – every visit to the pub, which is the heart of Coigach social life. Drinking is friendly, cordial, merry, excessive or wild, depending on the occasion. No shame or embarrassment is attached to it.

The difference between an alcoholic and a drunk, is that the drunk has a choice. Many in Coigach choose to be drunk once in a while, and I am no exception. Let me explain. I've already described drinking in rounds, where men take turns buying a round of whisky for everyone in their immediate group – sitting at a table, standing together at the bar, playing pool, whatever. Sometimes those groups get pretty big; many drams may appear at your elbow before it's your turn to buy a round. If you can even remember by that time. Sometimes you lose count, sometimes you just don't give a damn.

You don't want to leave the pub until you've stood your hand, of course. And by the time you've made it back from the bar with your tray of drinks, the group has grown – and the new arrival has brought his own round, of which you must betake a dram. Everyone prides himself in being known as a man who stands his hand. This gets a bit competitive after a while. It's almost like the potlatch tradition among the Kwakiutl of America's Pacific Northwest – a tradition of being generous to a fault. And generosity in a Highland pub is metered out in drams.

So being occasionally drunk, or legless, or pissed – depending on your chosen term – is not uncommon in Coigach. And if I'm trying to avoid that condition at the Fuaran or in the Summer Isles pub, yet still facing a formidable rank of golden whisky glasses, I'll sometimes pick up a dram, wander off to the loo and furtively pour it down the urinal. Not that this stratagem saves me from becoming drunk – it just helps slow the process and controls the damage. I have probably poured more whisky down the urinal in the Fuaran than I drink in a year in the States

Yes, there are alcoholics in Coigach, as there are almost everywhere. But most people simply enjoy their drink and still function quite well as citizens, parents, neighbors and friends. On ceilidh nights in Castlehill, folks come with whisky or ale to share around in the same convivial way they share songs. Once in a while, someone might fall asleep in a corner and have to be driven home by a neighbor, but misbehavior is never acceptable.

Ceilidhs usually evolve spontaneously, around closing time at the pub. As the call for last drinks approaches, one patron might casually ask another 'back to the house' for a dram or two – especially if the invitee happens to be carrying a musical instrument. Others will hear this and decide to come along for the fun. The word spreads quickly. There will be a last-minute crush at the bar as everyone buys bottles of whisky or ale for 'carry-out.'

Sometimes you don't even know where you're going. You just follow a parade of vehicles out of the car park and down the road, and wind up in someone's house. It doesn't matter, for neighbors and friends are always welcome. Strangers, too, so long as they have a song to sing or a tune to play.

One of the first ceilidhs we went to, Donnie Post who entered the house ahead of me opened a new bottle of whisky, crushed the thin metal cap in his fingers and threw it away. Why save the cap for a bottle meant to be emptied before that night was over? Bottles and ale cans become common property, placed on the kitchen table for all to enjoy. Everyone contributes, no one counts the cost.

While the roisterers crowd into the lounge and the singing begins, the hostess bustles about the kitchen making sandwiches or popcorn or anything she can find in pantry or fridge to feed the unexpected guests. In a pinch, children of the house and neighbors may be enlisted to help prepare and serve food. The night may last however long and no one goes hungry in a Highland home.

Actually, ceilidhs tend to inflict a degree of sobriety on me. When everyone else is singing or playing their fiddle or pennywhistle, harp or melodeon, I like to pretend that I'm playing music on my concertina. But the concertina has an edgy sound that's hard to conceal behind other instruments. And I have discovered that whisky in excess has the remarkable effect of moving my concertina buttons into new and unfamiliar places, causing the instrument under my fingers to emit totally unpredictable sounds. To keep the buttons in their place, I have to remain moderately sober through the course of the evening.

Moderately.

So – what do real Highlanders drink – at least in Coigach? Mostly, blended scotch whisky, no ice, a splash of water from the pitcher on the bar. Water is never ever added directly from a tap, but always decanted first into an intermediate container before pouring (carefully) into a glass of whisky. "Same again" is the common mixture of the two. Bell's and The Famous Grouse are popular, because they are there. And McEwan's ale. Single malt whiskies are for special occasions, and really seldom seen. Sherry is on offer in most homes, mostly popular among women.

There is a ritual aspect to whisky drinking. In a culture noted for hospitality, drams tend to be generous to a fault. There is the story told by an indignant Highlander who had been offered whisky by an Englishman. "He said, 'say when.' So I said 'when.' And the bugger stopped pouring!"

Even under the roughest conditions, people here are able to make the first dram seem like an occasion. When we take a break from the dipping or clipping at Achnahaird fank, Alasdair sets out his stainless steel drinking cups with all the care of a Paris sommelier and carefully wipes them clean before pouring out generous drams. Often he'll have a bottle of spring water on hand, as well, to temper the fiery liquid. And no one sips from his cup until all have drinks in hand, and raise them to each other with a ritual 'slainte mhath' and 'slainte mhor.'

There is also an unstated sense of – for lack of a better word – naughtiness, a secret wink and nod with every dram that says "we really shouldn't, but..." But we shall, anyway.

## *June 12th*

*We've now had about three weeks straight of gorgeous weather. I hate to think of leaving when it's like this.*

*Yesterday we went into Ullapool so that I could get my hair cut and permed. As usual it's too curly. I had Bill, Margaret and Ian over for supper last night – cooked two more rabbits Bill brought us the night before, and made a strawberry shortcake. A delightful evening!*

*This morning I gave Jack a haircut, made bread and walked down the road to Aileen's shop to get something to take back to the States with me. I haven't been able to find what I wanted for the kids. Oh well.*

*Aggie Ross was in her garden so we stopped to visit. What a beautiful day! Spent the afternoon having tea with Murdo & Joan.*

# A Small Tragedy

It was Simon Schoolbus who discovered the abandoned lamb along the roadside near Polbain. The tiny creature was half dead, unable to stand by itself, and starving. Simon reported his find to Wilf and Wendy, who took in the lamb and bottle-fed it; but no matter what they did, the tiny creature failed to respond well. They took the lamb – now called Simon after its first human benefactor – to the vet in Dingwall for a second opinion after an old time vet in Gairloch advised them to let it die. The younger man had more faith in science and gave Simon an injection that seemed to help.

The young lamb showed signs of recovery, but still had difficulty walking, so the Bells again took him for treatment in Dingwall – and at last Simon began to walk and play like the other lambs. Wilf and Wendy kept him in Murdo's pasture, and in time Murdo himself took on the daily task of feeding young Simon.

Perhaps his own affliction stirred a special sympathy for the stricken lamb. Every day, with great effort, Murdo would rise from his bed or from his chair by the fire, and prepare food for Simon. He could always count on the lamb to be by the door, or within call, and the young lamb grew handsomely with the daily care from the old man. In time, he became a sturdy and bright-eyed wether with a lovely coat, and Murdo looked forward each day to feeding young Simon.

But one day Joan noticed that Simon was having difficulty walking again. And the next day, Murdo found that Simon had little appetite and was stumbling. That evening, Simon was unable to move, and Joan bedded him down in the barn. The next morning the lamb was dead.

Distraught, Joan cast about for some way to dispose of Simon's carcass. Finally she found a burlap sack and pulled it around the lamb's body. She dragged the heavy burden down across the fields, over the stone dikes, down to the edge of the sea. There she weighted the sack and tied it tight and committed it to the dark waters, while Murdo sat by the fire alone in the house.

## June 14th

*I'm killing time at Heathrow Airport, after spending the last couple days visiting people and saying goodbye. Yesterday morning Anne Irish came over to pick up a painting I'd done of her house and say goodbye. Ian and Joy had us over for a lovely lunch after which we left for Inverness. Booked into our B&B and walked down to the hotel for dinner. We had a great day all told – but I didn't sleep at all – excitement I guess. We were up at 6:00 for an early breakfast and off to the little local airport.*

*It was a beautiful morning – emerald green fields against distant mountains – bright red poppies and golden gorse. There's a lovely castle that we didn't even know was there – we'll have to explore it one of these days. When we arrived in time for my 7:30 flight, we found that it was delayed until 9:45 – Grrr!*

*So we read the paper and had a cup of tea and cooled our heels for a couple hours. Oh well – at least that meant only 3 hours here at Heathrow. Jack's mother is meeting me in Chicago – I'm anxious to see her! It will be 3:00 a.m. our time when I hit Minneapolis. So I'll be a wreck – but what a joy to see my dearies again!*

# Peace

June 20th. "La commedia é finito" – the comedy is over. After 74 days of combat, the Argentine forces have surrendered, and everyone here is applauding. But when the curtain falls on a comic opera war, the fallen are supposed to stand up and take their bows. Not this time. Almost 900 British and Argentine soldiers, sailors and airmen have been killed in action. More than twice that many will bear scars for the rest of their lives. All because some foolish men didn't think Britain would stand up to dictators. Well, they aren't the first to make that mistake. I guess it counts as a win for 'our' side. At least I know Donnie Darling will be back to his old self once young Donnie comes home unhurt.

# Letter to Barb in America

I have been granted an extension of my visa for another twelve months. If the Immigration people at Heathrow don't want to deal with your extension when you return, I'm sure we can just send your passport in to the Home Office and refer to my file for a similar extension. The Home Office reference number is M478273, which may be of some use when you come back through London.

The novel is progressing, still more slowly than I'd like it to be, but I am pleased so far with what I've done. I hope someone else will be. I've been getting up at 6 every morning and writing until noon. The story seems to unfold itself, my major preoccupation being finding the right phrases to get it down on paper. Sometimes it's difficult to know if the writing is where it should be, in that lovely but elusive area between the obscure and the obvious. I catch myself writing things that needn't be written, and leaving unexplained events that are clear in my head but not in my story.

Of course, it hasn't been all work. A week ago last Saturday Donnie Darling asked me to go out in his new boat to bring in a pair of sheep that had been on Eilean a'Char for the past three years. I got down to the harbor at high tide (about 7 p.m.) to find Donnie and his youngest boy Innis trying to launch the new boat, a fiberglass 16-footer identical to Wilf's *Annabelle*. I went to help them and – as always seems to happen when I help Donnie – I stepped into the water over the top of my boot. We got the motor mounted and started, and Donnie headed for the jetty to pick up a fishing rod he was borrowing from Walton. Unfortunately, he had not yet figured out how to put the motor into reverse, so we rammed the jetty at a hellish clip. No apparent damage, however.

Then we headed out for Eilean a'Char, a small island between Tanera Mor and Glas-leac Mor. Donnie's debut as captain hadn't worked out too well, so he relinquished the helm to Innis, who could scarcely conceal his delight. Close in to 'Char, we shut down the motor and Innis rowed in while Donnie growled a running series of commands, "hard a-port, hard-a-lee, goddamit boy, back off, back off, hard a-starboard!" Despite his directions, we landed well and Donnie, his dog and I went up while Innis held the boat offshore.

The first ewe was sneaky. She ran over the crest of a hill, and when I topped it, she was nowhere in sight. Puzzled, I scanned the small, bare island; not a wooly figure in sight. Then I noticed the tiny white tip of a sheep nose protruding from the earth about 20 yards away. She was crouching down in a hole among the rocks, and leapt out to run again when she realized she'd been spotted. But she was so overloaded with three years' growth of wool that a little running pooped her out and she was quickly caught. We dragged her down to the shore, tied her three legs and rolled her off the rock into the boat.

The second sheep, however, fled across the island and halfway down a long sloping cliff above the sea, where Donnie and the dog trapped her. Innis and I brought the boat around, ready to receive the fugitive. Donnie carefully edged his way down the steep rock face while I scrambled up from below. His outstretched fingers barely reached the terrified yow when she exploded into frantic action. She ran out to his arm's length, spreadeagling the man across the slope. He clutched her scruff with one hand and gripped a knob on the rock with the other, holding on to both for dear life.

She began running in a huge circle above, beside, below and back up the other side. Around the knob at the center, Donnie was spinning like the hand of a fast running clock. "Let 'er go," Innis shouted from the boat. "I've got the bitch," his whirling father gritted through his teeth. On the ewe's second orbit, as she swung down toward the sea again, Donnie let her go. Propelled by fear, gravity and centrifugal force, the white missile shot past me, smacked into the water and bobbed to the surface just inches from the waiting boat.

With great effort, Innis hauled the waterlogged mass of writhing wool over the rocking gunwales. Donnie and I scrambled to the top of the cliff and made our way across to the landing place. As we motored back to Old Dornie with our exhausted captives, Donnie was grinning. "Wilf said we'd never get 'em off alive. Well by god, we've got 'em now!"

Predictably, the evening ended at the Fuaran. Two days ago Donnie brought me a huge fine piece of sheep's liver (which I have consumed with pleasure) and an immense roast, which I halved and stowed in the freezer. All told, it was a successful adventure.

Incidentally, when Donnie clipped the two sheep from Eilean a'Char, I also gave a 'hand' and maintained my perfect record with him. While attempting to bulldog the biggest one, I was thrown sliding across the muck – turning my working denims a bilious greenish brown. My consolation was a chance to see a remarkable fleece. Being on an island devoid of trees or dikes or fence posts on which to rub off each year's growth, the ewe had grown three complete layers into a massive mattress of wool. The fleece weighed about 15 pounds, heavier than a sack of five he had just clipped from some hill sheep.

# Clipping the Sheep

Where the single-track road to Achiltibuie comes out from between the mountains and reaches the sea, you'll see a beautiful white sand beach curving around Achnahaird Bay, and beyond it the hills of Coigach. Just past that beach an even smaller road turns off to the right, going through the hamlet of Achnahaird and circling the Coigach peninsula through Reiff, Altandhu and Polbain, to rejoin the Achiltibuie road at Badentarbat. At the edge of this road, just beyond the fork and over a wee stone bridge, stands an old drystone fank by a small flat green. It was here that I learned to clip hill sheep, using the traditional scissor-like shears called 'blades.'

In the way of progress, most of the world's sheep these days are sheared with electric clippers, using high-speed techniques developed and honed by Aussie and New Zealand shearers. Sheep raising is an industry Down Under; flocks are immense, and shearing is done by organized teams in huge sheds under controlled conditions. In a working day, a man with electric shears might divest several hundred sheep of their fleeces. Top professional shearers are celebrities, and teams of them follow the seasons around the globe to denude the sheep of the world. But not in Coigach.

Oh, they say that Boysie Sinclair tried to introduce the electric shears one year, but the technology never took hold. In the first experimental use, too many sheep were badly cut by the whirring blades. And the electrics clipped too close for local taste – not enough wool was left to protect the ewes from the driving rain, howling gales or burning sun that might afflict them at any season. And most of the local crofters, who might run as few as 50 sheep, and seldom more than 200, have seen no reason to spend the money. Besides, speed was the only real advantage of the electrics, and none could see the need for such unseemly haste.

The clipping is done at a leisurely pace, beginning in late June when the rise first begins to appear on the older ewes. When it happens, you can actually see a space opening close to the sheep's skin where the tightly compacted fleece is breaking away, held on by relatively few fibers. If the animal is not shorn at the right time, it might lose much of its fleece when it rubs up against rocks, dikes and fences.

A sheep with a good rise is a pleasure to clip, the back of the blades riding along the skin while the sharp edges click and slice easily under the dense fleece. Without a good rise, clipping is just a chore. And the timing of the rise is different on every ewe, so the pace of clipping varies according to which sheep are ready. Ewes with lambs don't get their rise until early July, the younger hoggs and gimmers might not be ready until late summer. Add to this the requirement that fleeces be well dry before clipping, the fact that the sheep live outdoors, and the vagaries of West Highland weather, and you can see that clipping is not done on a rigid schedule. Or any schedule at all. So my eagerness to learn the mysteries of this disappearing craft was much frustrated that first full summer in Coigach.

Being city-born and bred, and something of a Type A personality, I'm one of those irritating people who show up for a 7 o'clock dinner date at 6:59. This attitude does not fit well into the pace of life in the West Highlands. A crofter at the pub might say, "The weather's been dry – I might do some clipping this week."

"When?"

"Oh, in a few days..."

Consulting my calendar watch: "Tomorrow? Thursday?"

Of course, he can't say which day, because he doesn't know yet. It might be fine for clipping tomorrow. Or something else might come up. Or it might rain and put everything off to another week. "Och, it could be tomorrow if the weather holds..."

"What time should I be there?"

He's taken aback. "Well I have to gather them in first..." He's never been asked for a schedule.

"Will you have them in by, say, ten o'clock?"

Now, if the weather is fine, this crofter might set out with his dogs some time after breakfast to gather his sheep. Unless he needs to repair a fence to keep his chickens from being run over by tourists. Or a neighbor stops for a friendly chat. Or the missus needs him to drive to Ullapool for groceries. If and when he gets to the hill, his sheep may or may not be exactly where he thinks they should be. They may or may not cooperate. The same is true of the dog, which hasn't worked sheep for some weeks. Knowing all the variables, the crofter struggles to find an answer for this insistent American. "Well, it could be..."

"Great! I'll see you at ten!"

Of course, it would be pissing down rain the next morning.

But I have come to admire many of the crofters I met during the winter, especially Alasdair West, and I am determined to experience what I can of the crofting life before it disappears. So, awkward, insistent and wrong-footed as I am, and totally devoid of experience with livestock, I keep pressing for an opportunity to work at their side. I think most of them looked on me as a curious nuisance at first, but

West is the first to risk his sheep in my hands. And gradually, over the first summer, he has come to accept me as a useful helper.

My first job was catching. The catcher's job is to wade in amongst the crowding sheep, grab one by the scruff, drag it out of the pen and set it upright on its backside, ready to be clipped. This takes more effort than skill, although the woolly rascals are more elusive than one would think. At the Achnahaird fank, sheep are penned behind thick drystone walls, and wrestled out one by one onto the unfenced green. Lose your grip on a ewe, and she'll be off to the hill in a flash.

One catcher can serve three or four clippers, who bend over the sheep and click away with their blades until the fleeces fall away in one piece like thick woolen blankets. The denuded sheep bound away, amazed at their own lightness, while a roller – sometimes the crofter, sometimes his wife or another woman – gathers up each fleece and carefully folds and rolls it into a snug package, twisting up a rope of wool from the neck end of the fleece to tie it. The rolled fleeces are counted, then packed into a wool sack.

Clipping, then, is a group effort that might involve any number of people from the community. It can be brutally hard work, but a social activity as well – almost always done on a lovely dry summer's day, with helpers arriving and leaving at random, and frequent breaks taken for sandwiches, tea or a dram. The work is accompanied by a music of its own: rhythmic clicking blades, cries of gulls wheeling overhead, baaaing of penned ewes, waves on the distant shore, wind in the grass, and laughter provoked by sharp conversation. I think it is this, more than anything else, that makes the crofters reluctant to change to the whirring industrial haste of the electric clippers.

After a few catching sessions, watching the clippers at work, I asked to try my hand at clipping. It is a tribute to Alasdair's kindness that he didn't say no, although his teeth seemed to clamp on his pipe just a bit, and one furry eyebrow tried to back off the top of his head. He picked out an old crog with half her fleece missing to be my first victim, and carefully tied three of her legs together. "Always leave one leg free, that way they won't kick as much."

The blades he handed me were long, heavy and very very sharp. I cringed at the thought that one false click might whack a teat off the sheep's bulging udder, or send a leg o'lamb spinning to the turf. I knelt by the tied ewe and, lifting the fleece slightly, began taking tiny snips into the gap of the rise. "Don't lift the fleece," Alasdair growled, "you pull the skin up into the blades." Oh. "Keep the top blade away from the sheep, boy, and take a bigger cut or you'll never finish." Oh. He watched me for a while, then, apparently satisfied that his ewe was in little danger, went back to his clipping. I believe he finished four or five sheep before I was done snipping out my first pathetic broken fleece. Maybe six.

In the following week, I eagerly volunteered my dubious services wherever sheep were being clipped in Coigach. The crofters allowed me to snip at a few ewes with expendable fleeces; I suspect it was a crafty ploy to keep me busy so I wouldn't bother them. I was so dreadfully slow that one time Donnie Darling knelt by the head of a ewe I was clipping and fed her a handful of grass. "So she won't starve to death before you finish."

Ian Roll, Ian the Fencer, Kenny Stuart and Willie John were clipping sheep down at Achiltibuie one Saturday evening and I went down hoping to lend a hand. Well. Ahem. The first sheep I did had absolutely no rise – the natural separation of the fleece hadn't begun yet, and the fleece was tight as a Persian carpet. I hacked and sweated and wrestled the beast for ages, getting the poor fleece off in sorry bits and pieces. And when I finally let her go, she ran off with a big fleecy patch on her rump that I had missed completely.

I clipped another with almost identical results, except the second one decided I was finished before I did, and ran off with me clinging to her neck, much to the amusement of the others. Sheep #3 and #4 were patchwork jobs – since I was unable to get a whole fleece off anyway, I gave up shearing the ones with full fleeces and went after a couple of tatty half-bald yows. Naturally, these two had already gotten a decent rise (that's why they were losing their wool) and I had a much easier time of it.

The four sheep I did wore me out completely – the other men did thirty or forty that evening and were fresh as morning dew. In fact, I stumbled off about 9 p.m. when the midges came out, had a hot bath and went to the pub, but Ian Roll kept the others going down at the fank until 11 when the rain came. His wife Hectoria brought periodic picnics of tea, sandwiches, cakes, whisky and water throughout the ordeal, bless her.

One sunny day in July I joined a crew on a croft in Polbain, and Donnie Darling tied a fat, full-fleeced ewe for me. I was beginning to take bigger blows with the blades now, and confident I could handle the challenge. Unlike the veteran clippers, who stood bent over their sheep and controlled them with their legs and feet, I was still kneeling to one side of my hog-tied subjects and depending on the 3-leg tie to hold them down. Big mistake.

I had cleared the belly and crutch wool, and most of the ewe's right side, and was lifting the blanket-like fleece away with my left hand and clipping toward her backbone when she slipped her bonds and lurched to her feet. Her rising shoulder struck against the blades in my right hand and drove the point into my left arm. With a yelp I dropped the blades, which then jabbed into my left leg. The ewe took off across the field, trailing her long half-clipped fleece like a bridal train. Donnie swore, some of the others hooted and laughed – until they saw the blood gushing from my elbow.

Kenny Pest drove me first to the District Nurse in Achiltibuie, who sent us on to the clinic in Ullapool where I received four stitches and a tetanus shot from Her Majesty's National Health Service. The ewe survived the ordeal uninjured, although half of her beautiful fleece was lost. Donnie caught her and recovered the other half. I'm sure there was plenty of wry laughter at my expense among the crofters at the Fuaran that night. And maybe a few chuckles among the sheep as well.

After that I abandoned the treacherous three-leg tie and tried to clip standing over the sheep like my neighbors.

Hill sheep are small, tough, and understandably leery of people who have already twisted off their tails, pushed them into toxic chemical dips, stuck them with needles, forced medicine down their throats, pursued them with frightening dogs and separated them from their lambs. When dragged out of a pen, set on their backsides and accosted with sharp steel blades, they tend to resist. Clipping a fleece off in one piece while trying to hold a hundred pounds of writhing muscle and bone with one hand, and wielding the blades with the other, is no small feat. The real art of clipping lies not in handling the blades, but in controlling the sheep. Especially at Achnahaird, where the unfenced green invites escape to miles of open hill and mountainside.

This summer, Alasdair West's son Angus came home from university and, like I, was a newcomer to the art of the clipping. Our early attempts to manage unbound sheep at Achnahaird looked more like wrestling matches. Often we had to throw the blades aside and pin our opponents to the ground, man and ewe panting and eying each other with hatred. Sometimes we couldn't prevent a sheep getting to its feet, and only barred its escape by holding onto its neck and being dragged across the green under its belly, like Odysseus escaping the Cyclops. With time and experience we learned to use our feet and legs to hold our victims securely and keep them calm while we clipped away.

The regular crew at the green includes young Ali West, whose clipping skills are well ahead of mine and Angie's, and Marilyn, Coigach's only shepherdess and a willing apprentice to Alasdair. She is the wife of Hector the mechanic. Marilyn is a bonnie lass, dark hair and freckles and a merry laugh that is often triggered by our inept antics. She is a good hand at clipping, but prefers rolling fleeces – a skill she taught Barb during the long summer days at Achnahaird green.

Being right by the road, it is easy for anyone driving past to see the work being done. The Wests are well liked in Coigach, and there is always good crack and a dram or two for a willing hand. Stookie from Polglass often comes by to help, and Ali Beag, and others from time to time. The work is hard – even harder for us newcomers – and the end of the day finds us sweat-soaked and dung-stained, with aching backs, legs and arms.

One evening we were sitting bone-weary on the drystone dike across the road from the green, a light cooling breeze moving wisps from the clipping across the beaten grass. At last our labors were finished, the fank empty. Dozens of newly-shorn ewes grazed quietly nearby. The midsummer sun hung low on the horizon. Our arms and backs were aching, hands raw from gripping the blades, clothes stained and stinking from sweat, tar and lanolin. Alasdair had just wiped a few random wool fibers from his metal whisky cups and was passing the bottle when along the road came a stranger.

He was jogging along in a shiny blue stretch suit with white stripes on the legs, white athletic shoes and a white cap turned backward on his head. He smiled brightly as he jounced past, giving us a little wave and a cheery "Hi, guys!" Too tired to respond, we stared after the jogger as he disappeared up the road toward the beach tourist camp, his white heels flashing in the fading light. Alasdair's eyebrows shot up and he canted his head a moment, then he grinned. We all did. And raised our cups in silent sardonic salute to the benefits of healthy exercise.

# Independence Day

The Fourth of July is an American holiday, but there were no Americans in sight. Barb was back in the States visiting the kids, and I was feeling very much alone. The holiday had a hold on my mind. There should be parades, picnics and fireworks, bands playing, banners fluttering, old soldiers marching proudly past, Old Glory flying on the summer's breeze. There should be fun. Instead, the Fourth of July weekend brought nostalgia, maybe just a little homesickness, and the sense that something important was missing.

Independence Day was on a Sunday, and on Saturday morning I decided to make an occasion of it. When we left America, Barb's sister and brother-in-law had given us an American flag. I dug it from a drawer now, determined to see it fly. In search of a suitable flag pole, I went around to the old steading beside Castlehill and pushed open the weathered wooden door. Inside was a jumble of barrels, boxes and old fishing gear piled high against the stone walls. Sunlight filtered through a few holes in the corrugated iron roof and dust motes hung almost motionless in the beam that penetrated the gloom. The space was filled with the discards of generations, and time was held in a stillness I was reluctant to break.

I picked up an old black book, its covers warped with damp and its pages well-thumbed. It was a New Testament, written in Gaelic. It would have been read by lamplight, and given comfort on many a stormy night. A shallow wicker basket rested atop a tea chest – it had once held a long coil of fishing line, with baited hooks carefully arranged around its perimeter. Dried-out cork floats lay here and there, and brittle fishnets spoke of the sea. Curious iron tools with worn wooden handles hinted at work on the croft now past and forgotten.

In a wooden box, I found a complete set of iron cobbler's lasts. There were eight of them, red with rust, ranging in size and shape from a small child's foot to that of a large adult. No doubt many a father had labored in this steading to keep his children in shoes. I lined them up in the sun on the dusty window sill, the invisible marching order of a long gone family.

Back in a corner stood a long wooden oar, with half its blade split away. Here was my flag pole! I trimmed away the other side of the blade, forming the oar into a single shaft a good ten feet long. A length of light hemp cord retrieved from a nail on the steading wall would serve to bind the pole to the red gatepost in front of Castlehill. I was strangely elated as I marched down to the gate, attached the Stars & Stripes to the old oar and raised it into the westerly breeze.

The road was empty, and my only witness was a black-backed gull soaring high above Castlehill. If the bird was puzzled by what it saw, it was probably no more so than most of my neighbors would have been, for they don't make too much of a fuss about their flag. Standing erect, hand over my heart, I recited the old litany that had opened every school day when I was a child. And when I had finished, I had to wipe my eyes. It must have been the wind.

That afternoon I brought Murdo out for our usual Saturday pint. When we walked into the Fuaran, a ragged chorus of male voices rose in song. "Oh beautiful, for spacious skies, for amber waves of grain..." The musical key was mixed at best, and the performance sputtered out quickly – those were about all the words they knew – but it was enough.

Remote as Coigach is, the people here have connections long and strong across the Atlantic. In 1773, the ship Hector picked up 179 passengers from the shores of Loch Broom – many from Coigach families. After a long and harrowing crossing, they were set down in the wilds of Nova Scotia near the onset of winter to survive as best they could – and survive they did. By one estimate, there are more than 40,000 descendants of the Hector people now living in Canada and the United States.

But Coigach has even stronger and more recent connections to the United States. In the early 1900s, the western sheep industry was booming, and American ranchers needed men who knew how to keep sheep alive in the mountains. They sent recruiters to the Highlands, and more than a few young Macleods, Mackenzies, Campbells and Rosses crossed the Atlantic to herd sheep in Montana and Wyoming.

It was a harsh and lonely life, but the pay was good for that time. With nothing to spend it on in the mountains, a young man could accumulate a fair bit of cash. Some of the shepherds stayed on and settled into the new land, so that many in Coigach today keep in touch with uncles and cousins in America. The ones who came back brought American money and ten-gallon hats, and for their freewheeling slang came to be known as 'The Goddamns.'

Sunday, the Fourth, a lovely day, I went down to the Summer Isles pub. The tiny room was mostly filled with locals and humming with summer gossip. I surveyed the crowd – almost two dozen people – then pushed my way through to the bar. Ian the Fencer's wife, who worked at the hotel, was tending. "What are you having, Jack?"

"Thirty whiskies, please."

Her eyes widened. "Thirteen whiskies?!!"

"No. Thirty whiskies. Three zed. Thirty."

"Er...Bell's, or Grouse?"

"Either. Both. Whatever."

She set a tray on the back counter and counted out thirty glasses. Two by two, like a milkmaid working the teats of a cow, she pressed the glasses up to the optical dispensers below the inverted whisky bottles and drew the drams. People at the bar began to watch her rhythmic filling movements. Lines of golden whiskies appearing on a tray, and rank on rank of empties a-waiting, are bound to catch attention in a Highland pub. Heads turned, conversations paused throughout the room. By the time she set the last one down, the place had gone silent. All eyes were on us as she passed the tray across to me. I turned to the waiting crowd. "Who'll join me in drinking to American independence from the Crown?"

In the hubbub that followed, there were many toasts to the Fourth, to liberty, to America. And almost everyone commented on the Stars and Stripes in front of Castlehill. At the back of the room a group of locals began singing. "Oh, say can you see, by the dawn's early light..." It didn't go much farther – maybe "the rockets' red glare" soared out of their vocal range (as it does mine), more likely they just didn't know the rest of the words. How many Americans can finish "God Save The Queen"? Whatever the cause, it was a lovely gesture.

After the pub closed for the afternoon, Ken The Bread invited me up to his wee caravan in Polbain. He had some unexpected visitors he thought I'd enjoy meeting – two women from New Jersey. As a product of the Midwest, I confess that East Coast dialects, and especially Joisey, ain't my favorite forms of American English, but they were welcome on my ear that day! To celebrate, I shared with them my prize from that week's shopping trip to Inverness: a Fourth of July watermelon (actually, it was grown in Spain and was the smallest watermelon I'd ever seen, but it was delicious). We only lacked tasteless hot dogs, packaged buns and glaring yellow mustard to complete the traditional picnic.

That evening I brought out a shotgun borrowed from Bill Baxter at Old Dornie. The sea was quiet, the islands dark, and the sun hanging low and red above the hills of Coigach. As near to sunset as it gets in midsummer, I fired off 13 salutes – one for each of the original 13 colonies. The sound was swallowed by the gathering gloom; I doubt that anyone noticed. Then I took Old Glory down from the oar shaft, folded her gently and put her away.

That was the first-ever Independence Day celebrated in Coigach. It would not be the last.

### July 20th

*I had a good – if tiring – trip back. I got into Inverness about 8:30 p.m. and it was so good to see Jack again! It was light all the way home so we could enjoy the drive. Stepping out of the car and breathing the air here gave me an intoxicating rush – you can't imagine how sweet it is after being in the city and away from the sea!*

*The first few days I was back, I felt kind of down – I missed the warmth and affection of friends and family back in Minneapolis. But I've been busy every minute since I've come back. Summer here is lived at about twice the pace as the winter months. The place is crawling with tourists, salmon and lobster fishing are in full swing, the herring fleets are in, and there is always a musical program or dance going on in the village hall.*

# Murdo Moon and the Amazing Electronic Sporran

To understand what happened the other night in the Achiltibuie Village Hall when Murdo Moon was almost murdered because of an amazing electronic sporran, you have to know something about the role of the kilt in the Northwest Highlands – and something about Murdo Moon's little jokes.

Murdo is a tall, strapping young Highlander, likeable and pleasant in all aspects – when sober. But when the whisky gets the best of him – as often it does – he likes to entertain people. And his favorite joke, when in his cups, is to drop his trousers and bare his backside to all and sundry. What you might call a bum joke.

In an urban setting where people can pick and choose their social circles, Murdo Moon's little jokes might be cause for scandal and social ostracism. But in Coigach, where people are few and each person needs everyone else, folks are more tolerant of eccentricity. Thus Murdo's well rounded exhibitions are usually ignored, sometimes applauded, but never condemned. If there ever is comment, it might be along these lines: "Poor Murdo's looking a bit pale tonight." "Aye. But his complexion's improving."

It is always trousers he is dropping, because in the Northwest Highlands the kilt is worn only by pipers and drummers, wedding parties, and tourists pretending to be Highlanders. For locals in a land of ferocious biting midges, the leg-baring garment is not too practical. But for Murdo Moon, the kilt must be a matter of absolute fascination, as it would be a most convenient garment for entertaining folks with his favorite joke.

Fortunately, Coigach has other forms of entertainment. The Highland Arts Council subsidizes all sorts of performers to make the rounds of isolated villages, bringing culture to the benighted denizens. The Achiltibuie Village Hall has even been graced by such prominent folk artists as the Boys of the Lough and Battlefield Band.

On this particular night the Council had sent a rather puzzling offering: a quartet performing the tartan kitsch, "Scottish Musical Night" sort of program featured on coach tours for foreign visitors – hardly the thing for a hardcore West Highland audience. The ensemble consisted of a sweating, fumble-fingered accordionist; a terminally bored drummer; a tall, skinny dancer whose angular Highland flings gave her the look of a giraffe gone mad; and an off-key male singer in elaborate Highland dress.

What the group lacked in talent, they made up in costuming. The singer was a chameleon peacock, leaping behind the stage curtain after each song, to appear moments later in a different Highland outfit. As the program labored onward, his shirt-fronts became lacier, his belts wider, his kilts more imaginative – checks, stripes, designer tartans. And his sporrans – the traditional pouch hanging below the belt buckle and swinging suggestively over the kilt-wearer's privates – became larger, fuzzier, more outrageous.

At the far end of the long, narrow hall throughout the evening, in the darkness by the door, the usual collection of young local men were standing – stepping out to the car park now and again to down a dram or a can of McEwan's ale. Most of them had lost interest in the program, and were only hanging about in hopes of winning the door prize: a half-bottle of Bell's whisky. But one pair of eyes in that darkness was locked on the parade of wild kilts and flying sporrans. And even after many visits to the car park with his mates and enough "slainte mhaths" to stun an ox, Murdo Moon never lost focus on the objects of his attention. With a zipperless, bottomless kilt and sporran, what fine jokes he could play!

The accordion wheezed, the drummer thumped, the dancer whirled in a cloud of elbows and knees. And the audience fidgeted and – almost unheard of in the Highlands – consulted their watches. At the interval, many of the men quietly stepped out of the hall and departed for the pub. Those who stayed on for the second half clapped dutifully, perhaps hoping to urge the performers to a hasty end.

As the performance labored on, the singer's costumes became unimaginably brilliant. When the grand finale came at last, he pranced onto the stage in a blue, orange and purple pastel tartan kilt. And swinging boldly over his thighs was the longest, wildest, hairiest sporran ever seen, its silver clasp inset with amazing multicolored electronic lights that twinkled as he sang!

Even the most somnolent in the audience were startled into applause. And then, with the end of the music, came the moment the boys at the back were waiting for: the drawing for the half-bottle of whisky. The singer stepped to the front of the stage, his amazing electronic sporran winking wildly, and extracted a ticket from the box proffered by the hall committee chairman. Drum roll. "The winner is – 4371!"

No response.

He called out the number again. There was a murmur of speculation in the crowd. Perhaps the winning ticket holder had been among the many who had escaped to the pub during the interval. "For the last time," he announced, "number 4371!"

From the back of the darkened hall came a thick, blurry voice: "I win! It's me, I win!" The village crowd fell silent as the tall unsteady figure of Murdo Moon came stumbling down the aisle. There was not one soul in the audience who believed he had the winning ticket. Surely this was one of Murdo Moon's mad ploys.

The man up on the stage smiled, his white entertainer's teeth glittering almost as brightly as the lights in his sporran that winked as he cried, "Ladies and gentlemen, we have a winner!" He held forth a half-bottle of Bell's.

"Aye," hiccupped Murdo, "Here I come!" His legs were all at sea, as if the floor were tilting and heaving as he made his way to the front. Yet onward he came, determined, desperate, drawn like a moth to a strangely twinkling flame. That glorious kilt, the amazing electronic sporran were just at eye level now, and almost in reach. He lurched forward, outstretched fingers clawing past the singer's hand, past the waiting whisky bottle, groping for what he must have hoped was the real prize.

Perhaps he groped a bit too far.

Howling in pain and outrage, the singer dropped the bottle and clutched to protect his groin. Then his free hand clamped around Murdo's throat, intent on doing murder. Strong men sprang forward to pry them apart. Chairs fell, chaos erupted throughout the hall. Many feared for Murdo's life. More feared for the falling half bottle, which landed intact among the scuffling feet and promptly disappeared.

By the time the house lights came up and calm was restored, Murdo Moon had escaped into the night, wandering off on his own somewhere to dream of bright kilts and twinkling sporrans.

## July 28th

A few nights ago there was a group of folk dancers and musicians from a small town in Sweden giving a program. It was really fun because the whole second half consisted of dances that they did with the audience – so we got to learn Swedish line and circle folk dances.

The pub is terribly crowded now with all the visitors in – we've had good times there, but sometimes it's so packed that it's unpleasant. People enjoy the tourists enjoying themselves – but look forward to the fall when the pub and the roads are their own again.

Jack helped Peter take in his prawn creels for the season, and was given a large box of prawns, which we cooked up and took over to Bill's house the next day for lunch. He had been out that morning and found five lobsters and two large crabs in his creels – so we shared a fabulous lunch (there were seven of us) of lobster, crab, prawns, bread and a big salad. Peter also gave us a huge salmon – so our freezer has a fair supply of seafood.

## August 4th

Much of our time has been spent helping various friends with the clipping. Jack started out catching sheep for the shearers – and ended the season doing quite a lot of clipping himself. It's been our favorite part of the year – it's hard work, but there's lots of laughter and fun too. Our favorite place to go for clipping is at Achnahaird – both because of the glorious scenery there, and because the people are well organized, do everything well, and really care for their animals.

We stop every once in a while for a beer or a dram – and for tea with sandwiches and cakes. At Achnahaird the pens are right next to the road and tourists stop and look and ask questions and snap pictures. At one point a visitor pointed at Jack and said, "Now, there's a big Highlander!" They'll take their photos home and feel they've captured the natives at work!

*There's such a pleasure in those days – hard physical work, with the sun warm on the skin and the cool sea breeze – the smell of wool and the lovely sound of the shears, with time out to sit in the shade of the stone wall and look out at the beautiful sand beach, the sea and blue mountains in the distance.*

## August 8th

*We worked one day at the shearing for the Inverpolly estate, just up the Wee Mad Road from Coigach – a very different experience! They run about 1200 sheep and have two full time shepherds. The shearing takes place in a huge shed, with three professional shearers from New Zealand hired in – it looks like a scene from "The Sundowners" with all the men, women, children and dogs involved and working like mad.*

*The sheep are penned inside the shed and it gets noisy with the bleating and the sound of the electric shear motors and the people yelling to be heard above it all. I tended the gate and Jack did catching – it took five catchers to keep the shearers supplied. They're fantastically fast – never stop – and can do about 50 sheep per hour each. The kids worked hard sweeping up the wool, carrying fleeces to the rollers and bringing the tar bucket to patch the wounds whenever one of the sheep got cut.*

*The wool bags were hung from the ceiling and one of the smaller kids would climb into the bag and pack the fleeces underfoot as they were tossed up. During the few rest breaks the kids would slide down the huge piles of wool bags on bag sleds. It was a beautiful day, sunny and warm, but cool in the shed.*

*After the last sheep was clipped we all went down and washed in the river – then up to the farmhouse for a fantastic meal that the estate women put on for the shearers. We sat around the table on planks set on fish boxes and ate like piggies – starting with soup, then cold salmon and ham with salad, hot turkey with dressing, sausages, potatoes, carrots, peas, beans, gravy and trifle for dessert – followed by tea, coffee, cookies and buttered scones with jelly.*

# Reflections on the Inverpolly Shearing

It was busy, it was chaotic, it was fun. But the big shearing at Inverpolly brought home to me the special nature of clipping with blade shears, and a sense of what we are losing as we gain economies of time and scale.

Certainly machine shears are faster than the blades. Certainly they make possible the harvest of wool from great numbers of sheep in a short time, with relatively few workers. The speed of the New Zealander crew was awesome. But work it was and pleasure it wasn't and the slow pace of clipping at Achnahaird suits me better. Suits the sheep better, too.

For the sheep, the slant of the blade shears in hand tends to leave light ridges of wool on the skin that protect them from the sun – should it ever come out – and the cold rain, which is always more likely. The machine shears trim flat to their thin pink skins. And sometimes deeper, for the teeth of the speeding blades can chew nasty multiple wounds into those fragile skins, and a man in a hurry makes more mistakes. Blade shears can cut a sheep, too, but cleaner, less often, less deep.

For the man, blades or shears, the work is the same: hard sweating, arm jerking, back bending labor. But while the machine man is measured by speed and paid by the boss for numbers on a wee metal counter, the blade clipper works at his own pace, and for himself or his friends. The one works in dust and motor noise and the vibrating kick of his hand-piece; the other hears laughter and talk and the cries of the wheeling gulls, and feels the satisfying snick as his blades come together.

I guess that where time and numbers are the most important equation, the machine men will always win hands down. But if a different kind of time and fellowship are tallied together, blade clippers will continue to hold their own.

*August 15th*

One of the most beautiful days we've spent – a trip out to Priest Island, the furthest and most beautiful of the Summer Isles. Our friend Bill has a good-sized boat that he uses for lobster fishing so we packed a picnic and went off for the day. We checked his lobster

*creels on the way out – it's over an hour's run to Priest. No one lives on the island and the only landing is against the high rocks on the south side – you can't really land in bad weather at all.*

*At one time, many years ago, a man in this area was discovered stealing sheep. Local justice decreed that he be marooned on Priest with a few sheep – and there he lived out his life. The remains of his house are still there. The island is now owned by the Nature Conservancy and some rare birds (great skuas and stormy petrels) nest there.*

*There's a chain of freshwater lochs running down the middle of the island and when we got to them we ran into a family who had been camping there for the week. The man's an ornithologist and comes here every year to net and band the petrels. The birds come out at night and the man and his wife string up a net about the size of a volley ball net to snare the birds. They'd banded two or three hundred birds so far.*

*We went back to the beach, built a fire and had our picnic, after which we went to explore the outlaw's house and find a place to swim. The three guys went swimming in one of the lochs. I chickened out and lay in the sun instead. The heather felt like a featherbed and we all ended up sleeping. In the evening we took the long way home through the islands and ended up at the pub. A more idyllic day I can't imagine.*

# Social Backbone: The Single Track Road

From the window behind my typewriter I can watch the road below. Not 'watch,' really – it's just that I subconsciously log the comings and goings even as I work on the novel. The road is my local newscast, my daily gazetteer, my finger on the pulse of Coigach.

I'm aware that Donnie Darling just drove past on his way to the Fuaran. I see (and hear) Kenny Pest buzzing down to Achiltibuie on his motorcycle. And Jim Muir and Ken the Bread heading up to the harbor in Jim's blue pickup, with creels and rope in the back, going out fishing for the day. Ah – Margaret Baxter's speeding up to Old Dornie, they must have renters coming. And Jimmy Mackay's truck is on its way to Inverness. Everyone in Coigach drives or walks on the narrow little single track road that runs around the peninsula and past the red gate of Castlehill. And everyone who isn't on the road takes note of everyone who is.

The road is our link to the world beyond, bringing us good things and necessary. A fish man comes around once a week; we can buy lovely kippers for our Sunday breakfasts. The coal truck rumbles through as well, and a man black with dust brings bags of soft Polish coal up the hill to dump in the shed by our kitchen door. On Wednesdays, the Royal Bank of Scotland van makes a regular stop below the cluster of houses at our end of Polbain. We walk down to the road where our neighbors are queuing up to do their banking. Inside the back of the van is a quaint little teller's cage where we can cash checks, pay bills and get the latest word from Ullapool.

It is a good road, smooth and black and well tended by the orange-clad county road crew. Being on the road gang is one of the few wage-earning jobs for men in Coigach, and it's as much an Old Boys' Club as a working outfit. Yes, they do work. They repair cracks and holes and bridges and culverts along the road's 28 mile length, and plow it open to the A835 when heavy snow clogs the intersection at Drumrunie. But many an hour is also spent drinking tea and playing 'Snap' in the cab of the county truck. Jobs on the road gang are at a premium, and an applicant's compatibility with the rest of the crew is an important job qualification.

The road itself is just wide enough for one vehicle, with a wider place every hundred yards or so, marked by a white reflective diamond on a post, where two cars can pass each other. There is a protocol to driving single track roads. If you see a vehicle coming up in your rear view mirror, you pull off to the left at the next passing place to let the faster car go by. When a car approaches from ahead, there is a delicate dance wherein the car nearest to a passing place pulls off.

Most times, drivers are overly polite, as if points in heaven are given to whoever first gives way to the other. Flashing your headlights is the conventional signal that you want to wait while the other driver comes ahead. Sometimes, both vehicles may pull off into passing places a hundred yards apart and flash their headlights at each other in an automotive version of "After you, Alphonse" and "No, you first, my dear Gaston!"

Of course, there are exceptions. Like the day I was driving back from Ullapool with some groceries and a copy of the weekly Ross-Shire Journal. I came to a long, straight, open stretch with a passing place at each end. The road was empty when I drove past the wide space at my end, but a moment later I saw a large car appear over the distant crest. No problem, I thought; there is another passing place between us. Plenty of opportunity for him to pull off.

But the car kept coming. Right past the obvious passing place. Straight on toward me. Surely he'll see me and stop, back up, let me by. But on he came. It was a big beautiful Bentley, a majestic machine that reeks of money and – in Britain – assumed privilege. I braked to a stop in the center of the single track road. The Bentley drew up close, looming over my battered little Mini like the Titanic over a tugboat.

The driver stared down imperiously, reached toward his windscreen with the back of his hand pointing downward, and flicked his fingers at me as if shooing a bug. The gesture clearly meant 'back up.' To show my admiration for his skill at sign language, I communicated in kind. The man's expression changed from boredom to irritation, and he flicked his hand again. 'Back up.' Same to you, I silently replied.

Now his face went red. He gave a long blast with the Bentley's horn, which shook the Mini as would the Last Trump. But by this time, I was really enjoying our little mime and determined to continue in the same silent spirit. I smiled at him, picked up the Ross-Shire Journal from the seat beside me, unfolded it ostentatiously and began to read. When, at the end of the first article, I looked up, the Bentley was sulking its way backward toward the last wide place it had passed.

I drove slowly up the road, smiled and tipped my cap politely to the Bentley's driver as I went by. He responded with a vigorous two-fingered salute, a British gesture that I believe has something to do with Henry V's victorious archers at Agincourt. Perhaps he thought I was French.

There is, by the way, a rhythm to driving the single track road.

Slowing down, speeding up, weaving around its curves is almost a musical performance, with accelerandos and legatos, capriccios and allegros, half notes and rests. I can play it in my mind even now, and almost drive the road blind. Some might even say that I've done so, on certain nocturnal occasions.

Walking the single track half a mile from Castlehill to Polbain Stores can take about 10 minutes. Or an hour. Or half a day.

It's not like on your city streets, where you are always passing people you don't know, cars you've never seen. You avoid eye contact and hurry on your way, for you are all strangers with little or nothing in common. In Coigach, everyone you meet along the road is a neighbor with mutual interests and common cause. When you walk, everyone driving the same direction stops to ask if you want a lift. Or wants to know how that batch of bread turned out, or if you've seen so-and-so, or will you be going to the whist tonight?

If a neighbor is tending his garden or painting a fence or patching a roof as you come by, he stops, wipes his brow and welcomes the opportunity to take a break and have a bit of a natter with you. "Here, let me show you..." "Have you heard about..." "Will you come in for tea?" If Murdo William is operating his JCB backhoe in the ditch along the way, he'll shut it down for a word or two. Joy Macdonald may show you something in her garden. If Jim Muir is repairing creels by his little Nissen hut, he'll greet you with a wide grin and maybe a story. Should Donnie Darling be moving sheep along the road, you'll pass a bit of time about the weather. Then Aggie will ask you in for tea. And there goes the afternoon.

I remember once when I was walking down to Achiltibuie and Jim's little pickup was coming the other way. He stopped in the middle of the road, and we were having a pleasant chat when a carload of tourists came along and drew up behind him. Jim was telling one of his tales, and a good one it was (although lost to memory now). Another unfamiliar car stopped behind the first one, and then a third. Jim's story went on. Now one of the cars sounded a horn briefly. I asked, "um, shouldn't we let these people by?"

"Oh, they're only tourists on holiday," he laughed, "all in a big hurry to relax." Another toot. Jim leaned out the window, gave the tooter a friendly wave, and continued his story. Someone in the third car back yelled something inaudible out his window.

"Um, Jim..."

"Don't worry. We're just locals, they expect this." In his own time, Jim concluded his yarn. I was still laughing as he put the truck in gear and pulled away. Behind him followed four cars – from the looks they gave me as they passed, they could have been steam-powered.

## August 22nd

*Now that the shearing's over I'm hoping to get some painting done. Jack's doing pretty well on his novel – although it's not finished yet. We read a book some time ago by an old Irish crofter, who every time he went off with his cronies to the pub or to enjoy some unexpected pleasure instead of doing the work he was supposed to be doing, would say to his mother, "This is a day in our lives – and it will never come again."*

*We've sort of adopted that as our motto – and every time we go off to the clipping, or out on the sea, or off to the islands instead of writing and painting, we tell ourselves "This is a day in our lives" – and it's true!! Who knows what the future will bring? Right now we are doing things that we would never have imagined – and every day is a joy and an opportunity to experience something new. Who said middle-age is boring?*

The Coigach flocks have been denuded, the great wool bags are stacked in barns around the community, and we're sitting out the August gales. The loch is busy with herring seiners right now, and soon the mackerel trawlers will follow. Tourists from Germany, France, Holland, Belgium and Sweden clutter the roads and have great difficulty with the passing protocol on our single-track routes. When the gales aren't howling, the air is full of midges – gnat-sized beasts with the appetites of piranhas and the teeth of tigers. They make Minnesota mosquitoes seem absolutely benign by comparison.

## August 22nd

*My goodness – a lot has happened in the last few weeks! August 5 was Alasdair West's retirement party at the Fuaran. Jimmy, Ruth and the kids came from Portmahomack to spend the weekend with us and play at the party. Ali Beag and Davy West also played – plenty of music! We all ended up at West's for a ceilidh until 5:30 a.m., and Pete played for dancing outside.*

*Had a good session next night at the Fuaran, after which a whole gang came in for a ceilidh and we ended up singing and playing 'til 5:00 a.m. again. Sunday everyone came for breakfast – then off to the Summer Isles for some music in the afternoon – then back here for a picnic and lazy afternoon on the lawn. Jimmy, Ruth and the kids left in the evening – a really great weekend was had by all.*

# Autumn

## September 7th

Well – we've come to the end of our first year in the Highlands and seen the whole cycle of seasons. It seems strange to live in a place where the life of the community is so dependent on that cycle. In the city, fall meant hanging storm windows, raking leaves and getting the house ready for winter – but work went on as usual and life didn't change much (other than getting a bit more muffled in wool and down).

Here there's a real feeling of change. The summer herring and salmon fishing is over and the mackerel fleets are trawling back and forth down the loch again. The last of the prawn fishers have taken in their gear to avoid damage by mackerel fleets and the salmon nets are being cleaned and dried (that is they'd dry if it ever stopped raining.).

## September 10th

We spent Wednesday last week helping Alasdair gather and dip 260 lambs. The dipper at Achnahaird is a small concrete tub that stands about waist high, and no ramp to lead the sheep into it! Each one had to be caught, lifted on its back and dropped upside down into the dip. It was hard and dirty work – but fun. They had to be dipped before going to market.

On Thursday the truck came and picked up most of the local sheep and took them into Dingwall for the auction. It was much more fun going to the sale this year, knowing the work that went *into those lambs; and most of the shepherds are now friends so the prices they got meant something to us. Everyone was quite happy with what they got (Alasdair and John Alec did best – £31 for top wether lambs).*

*The weather has been wretched – gales and rain for the most part. One night we had a horrendous gale come up suddenly from the south and it caught one of the local boats out with a fishing party. They couldn't get back to the pier – or onto the harbor mooring. So all night long, while some of the local men kept in contact by radio, they motored round and round the harbor trying not to hit anything. Finally, about 6:00 a.m. they could see enough to snag the mooring and smaller boats could go out and get the men off.*

*The nights are getting longer and there's a feeling of drawing in – the community is closing up again. There are still quite a few visitors about – but somehow there's a change in the place. Jack is locked in his room putting together the final draft of his book. Every once in a while he crawls out for a meal or a distracted few minutes at the pub. He'll have it finished in a couple weeks – then comes the strain of trying to sell it.*

# Farewell to the Mini

Our little Mini has gone to the knacker's yard. It was due for the annual MOT safety test, and a pre-test inspection by our friendly, low-cost local car-fixer indicated that it would cost me about £250 just to pass the test – and that would still leave me with a badly rusting car. So we went back to Dingwall and traded it in on a younger, larger and apparently much healthier Volvo 66.

Americans will not have seen a Volvo 66, of course – they do not bring them into the US. It is, in fact, a Dutch car, which was known as the DAF before Volvo bought the company in 1975. I've had a secret desire to own a DAF for many years. It first came to me back when all of the cars in the US were given macho model names like Tiger, Panther, Eagle, Hawk, Mustang, etc. Courageously bucking the trend, DAF called their top model the Daffodil. Along with its quirky name, the DAF also has a unique drive system that uses variable-ratio belts and pulleys rather than gears. When you step on the accelerator, the engine speeds up first, and the car gradually catches up. Sounds a lot like a sewing machine, really, but it seems to work pretty well.

Anyway, since we now have a comfortable long-distance car (driving the Mini was like a long session in the tumble-dryer), we may take a month's trip down through France and northern Italy come October.

## September 15th

*Last weekend Donnie Darling and Mary gave a party for their son, who is home on leave after serving in the Falklands on HMS Broadsword. We all brought food and different people from the village entertained – very informally – and they brought in a disco outfit from Ullapool so the kids could dance. The feast was fantastic and a good night was had by all – except the guest of honor who was too embarrassed to come (he's a really nice young man – but rather shy).*

# Space

I grew up on Chicago's densely populated South Side, in a third-floor walk-up apartment. My father and mother had the one bedroom, my sister slept on a Murphy bed in the living room, and I had a studio couch in the dining room. The stairwell was always redolent of our neighbors' cooking; fortunately, ours was a mostly Jewish neighborhood so it usually smelled delicious. I played kick-the-can and baseball and football in city streets and alleys, where the goal line could be a '47 Chevy, the pitcher's mound a sewer lid and out-of-bounds was anybody's window.

In the city, we knew where it was safe and where it wasn't at what hour of the day or night. We knew everyone who lived in our building, a few more on our block, one or two on the next street – those were the boundaries of our 'community.' Our mother taught us to walk purposefully, don't talk to strangers and avoid eye contact that might invite danger. Try not to be alone on the street at night. Be wary.

Weather came at us through the filter of surrounding buildings, or down through the pale brown haze of city air. When the wind was just so, our nostrils were assailed by the infamous Chicago stockyards – as close to livestock as ever I cared to be.

I'm telling you this because I want you to understand how special Coigach is to me, every hour of every day we live here.

Coigach is space. From our doorstep I can see way down to the northern tip of Skye, forty miles away, and west to the Outer Hebrides. My eyes rest on islands and mountains and ships at sea, open fields and wave-washed shores and white sheep grazing on purple-heathered hills. I watch patches of sunlight following black squalls of rain racing up Loch Broom and over the Dundonnel hills, feel wind as it comes from the cloud-scrubbed sky, unsullied by smokestacks, untempered by intervening cities.

No day here is ever the same, no day is taken for granted.

The community I grew up in was circumscribed by city blocks. Now my community is the Highlands, and people scattered for miles around seem closer to me than people across the alley in

Chicago. Where neighborly favors were once exchanged along a corridor or up a stairwell, they now pass readily across a peninsula or around a mountain.

When your eyes are accustomed to scanning the world for miles, anything less seems restrictive. Ian Roll went south recently to visit relatives in Skye, and I asked him what he thought of the island. The big man pondered for a moment. "Well, I can't say I cared for it," he concluded. "Too many trees."

"Too many trees?"

"Aye. You couldn't see in any direction for the trees. And you just don't know what's going on behind them."

## November 10th

*At 9:00 this morning the power went out with a flash and a bang – also the phone. It's now 4:10 p.m. and I am writing this by firelight. There's been a terrific gale blowing since last night and the hail has come down so heavy it looks like snow on the road. We went into Ullapool this morning and had breakfast at the Fisherman's Mission – then did some shopping there and in Lochinver. Peter and Sally were supposed to come over for supper tonight – but if the power stays off much longer we'll have to go over there!*

*I've been wrapping Christmas presents to send off to the States. They should all go out this week and I still have most of them yet to buy.*

## November 16th

*Terrific gale blowing today. They've had to give us a new phone after the last storm knocked the electricity out. We had to make coffee on the camp stove and toast in front of the gas heater. The power came on in time for supper though.*

*The roof's still leaking – even after Jack re-tarred it yesterday. Now what? Don't know! Peter came over last night with a two pound chunk of smoked salmon. What a treat! How nice to have neighbors like that! Peter and Sally have a new baby – named her Rebecca – and Christopher is growing into the role of big brother.*

## November 18

*I've been having some health problems lately so this afternoon I went down to the village hall for the doctor's weekly "surgery." No one makes an appointment – you just go down and if you're there, the doctor will see you. So I took my place in the queue of wooden chairs lining the wall and waited my turn. Everyone looks at one another and wonders what could be wrong – but most are too polite to ask. So we all sat and nattered away until our turns came up. The nurse at the desk only asked my name and address – no forms to fill, no demand for proof that I had insurance and could pay the bill. The doctor said I should see a specialist in Inverness and that he will make an appointment for me.*

## November 19th

*A gale is still raging outside. The Department of Agriculture tups have been brought up for breeding and are probably wondering why they've been brought to such an awful place. They'll figure it out when they're put to the ewes! It's the beginning of a new sheep cycle that will end next fall with the sale in Dingwall.*

*I just finished baking a cake for Donnie Post's retirement party tonight. Hopefully we'll be taking Joan and Murdo for the presentation anyway. It should be fun.*

## November 20th

*Now that Donnie Post is no longer the postman, he'll revert to being Donnie Roll. And young Ali West will take his place and become Ali Post. These shifting names used to confuse us, but now that we know the people it's all perfectly clear – I think.*

*Murdo didn't come to Donnie Post's party at the Village Hall – his eyes were bothering him – but Joanie came and had a grand time as usual. She stayed 'til the end, which was about midnight. There was a program from 8:30 – 12:00. First Donnie was presented with a chair (recliner) and a cassette deck as an appreciation gift. Then there was a performance by the Last*

*Postman's Band (Simon, Ali & Gillis), followed by pipers, singers (all in Gaelic) and the kids' chorus.*

*Donnie and his brother Ian Roll sat up in front, all dressed up, and managed somehow during the program to get well oiled by the end of it – how I don't know! Afterwards we joined a group in the back room for a party, and danced and sang until about 3:30 a.m. It was a great night! Turns out the Manager is quite a good accordionist.*

*I've come to appreciate the Manager. He's quite attentive to Murdo on pub Saturdays – sits with him and talks when everyone else goes up to join the crowd at the pool table.*

## November 28th

*Well – here it is the end of November already. Thanksgiving has come and gone and the Christmas season looms on the horizon. I can't cope with the swift passage of time – it seems like I just got back from the States.*

*Our second Thanksgiving went like clockwork – Joan and W&W came again for turkey and all the trimmings (including pecan and pumpkin pies). We had a lovely evening and for once the electricity and water were both on all day. We had no water the day before – a main broke at Badentarbat – so I had misgivings, but we lucked out this time. I had some canned pumpkin and cranberries left from last year, and found pecans in the health food store in Inverness. No one here has ever had pumpkin or pecan pie, poor deprived people! Most don't even know what they are. They also get Thanksgiving and Independence Day mixed up and are always asking us if we have turkey on the Fourth.*

# Winter

## December 8th

*The days when the tups were first turned out were lovely. Ian Roll and Donnie Darling just agreed on who got which tup – no drawing lots this year. Ian marked the bellies of his tups with different colors the way they do in the borders – the wet paint marks the backsides of the ewes they have serviced, so he could see which tup was working best. Donnie thought that was new-fangled – not for him, no sir!*

*Jack spent several days helping Donnie and the Manager move and sort sheep. After a year of treating us as if we didn't exist, the Manager has opened up – and talked and talked and talked. Jack wonders if it wasn't better before. Anyway – it's another barrier down.*

*Jack has had no luck so far finding an agent or publisher to read his manuscript and is getting a little depressed about it. It's obviously a lot harder to get into that game than he thought. The thing is not to lose heart and give up before the right response comes along – but it's hard in the face of rejection slips. He hasn't had to deal with that in all his years of freelance script writing.*

## December 10th

*Father Brady has died of a massive heart attack. He was found dead one morning. A horrible shock for us all – but especially for Anne Irish. We went to his requiem mass in Inverness. It was very hard – and harder to think he's gone! He was so full of life, and song, and funny stories. Jack says he's probably in a pub in purgatory, waiting for a rabbi and a minister before approaching the pearly gates!*

## December 18th

*We went off to Glasgow on the 15th, stopping in Inverness for me to see the gynecologist. He said there is nothing seriously wrong, but I will need a D&C, so I'll have to go into the hospital for a few days in January. Yuck. Still no talk about money.*

# Second Christmas

A week before Christmas, came a knock at the door. There on the threshold stood a solemn-looking Iain Campbell. "I – I'm so sorry, Jack," said he, wringing his hands. "I was driving through the pine plantation near Muir of Ord last night, and it jumped out in front of the car and I accidentally killed it."

Before I could respond, he drew me by the arm through the doorway. There, leaning against the side of the house, was a beautiful Christmas tree. Iain's eyes were dancing with mirth. "I thought you wouldn't want the poor thing to go to waste."

Iain's gift reinforced the tradition of Christmas celebration we had introduced to Castlehill last year. Now the celebration is growing. With an empty guest room and a spare bed in Barb's studio, our house has become a welcoming haven for itinerant musicians, and we are becoming more and more involved with folk music. Some of Pete Taylor's musician friends are showing up at the Fuaran these winter nights, entertaining the locals and, after closing time, contributing to the quality and frequency of ceilidhs in our home.

Jimmy, a raucous redhead who works on North Sea oil rigs, belts out defiant songs from Jacobite days and the Red Clydeside, backed by his own guitar. Lovely Christine, from over the mountains in Tain, plays haunting traditional Celtic airs on harp and fiddle. Caroline provides percussion on bodhran and side-splitting humorous lyrics. Jovial Jan, the big Dutchman who runs the Achiltibuie youth hostel, plays bass

guitar and recorder. Pete, of course, plays and sings everything. Barb happily strums her guitar for this eclectic repertoire, while I quietly hum my two-note vocal range – one sharp, one flat.

Wendy Stewart and Alan James, visitors whom we first heard in the Fuaran last Christmas, have returned and become good friends. Her nimble fingers weave musical magic on a clarsach – the traditional Celtic harp – and lively Cajun tunes on an English concertina. Alan accompanies with guitar and pennywhistle, and both are lovely singers. Friends from Coigach – Irish Anne and Iain, Pete Taylor, Peter and Sally, Murdo William, Donnie Darling, and anyone else with a tune to play or a song to sing – or nothing more than an appreciative ear – contribute to the joyful hours as we play the long winter nights away.

## December 28th

*Christmas has come and gone – so fast it's over! We've had a lovely week. Friday night was the Village Hall carol service that Anne, Nessie, Rosie, Leslie and I had arranged. We sang carols, did a reading of the Christmas story, and served punch, tea and clootie dumpling. I was amazed the whole thing got off the ground at all – it was a bit disorganized but everyone seemed to enjoy it.*

*Jim & Aileen left us a gift of a bottle of wine and some truffles in our car! And when we got home we found a bag outside the door with two presents and an anonymous note: "from Santa with love." Inside were two beautiful coffee mugs filled with chocolate truffles! Joan came up and brought us a fresh chicken, a bottle of sherry, and a nice wallet for me. I ran into Ali Post on the road and he had our package from Mom & Dad – kitchen towels, T necks, wild rice packed in newspaper comics and magazines.*

*On Christmas morning we had croissants and fruit – then off to see Joan & Murdo and give them their presents and have a dram and sherry. Met Anne at the shed and went off to Ullapool for church. I really missed Fr. Brady – but it was nice anyway. When we got home we went over to W&W's for dinner, which was delicious from the turkey to plum pudding. Afterwards we had coffee and Bailey's by the fire and exchanged gifts. A thoroughly lovely day! We went home and took naps – made transatlantic phone calls – and then went to Anne's for a drink and visit. Home to bed by 3:00 a.m.*

# Now Where?

### January 4th

*Goodness, how time flies! Here it is another year and I must say the last one was a blue ribbon, gold star year for us – but this one holds some fears for the future. I wonder where we'll be next New Year. Who knows?*

*The last few days have been a mad whirl of celebration – I'm amazed we survived it! Friday was New Year's Eve. Pete came and picked up the harp and guitar he'd left and we had tea at Joan and Murdo's in the afternoon. In the evening we went to the pub – it was a great night there. Pete and his group were playing – concertina (which seems to fascinate Jack), guitar, mandolin, pennywhistles, flute, melodeon, fiddle – and Kenny Stuart played his pipes. Everyone was there and it was fun.*

*At closing we went over to Peter and Sally's to see the New Year in – then to Campbell's, Sinclair's, West's and Calum's and enjoyed it all immensely – until I started feeling bad and had to go home about 5:00 a.m.*

*New Year's Day I felt absolutely horrible – evidently got a touch of flu on top of a whopping hangover – but the beginning of Hogmanay is no time for the faint of heart. About 3:00 Donnie came by, and then Anne and Iain. We had some soup cooked over a gaz stove (no electricity) and a nice visit. Then off to Joan and Murdo's to first foot – at which point I collapsed and had to go to bed again.*

*Sunday I felt better. W&W came for the morning and we went to see Lance & Di in the afternoon, then Peter Davis, Vi Wilding,*

*Howard and Ailsa Seth-Smith, then home for dinner after which
a bunch of people came over for a few hours. Then all of us off to
Island View council houses to visit, then on to Donnie & Mary's
and after the pub closed John Alec, Catriona, Neil and Kay and
kids came over and stayed 'til 3:00 a.m.*

*Today we visited Aggie (she gave us nice gifts – hankies for Jack
and a tea-tray scarf for me!). Then to Jim Muir's and home for
dinner. Tonight Pete Taylor's band will be at the pub – so of course
we'll go along.*

## January 12th

*Another day of deadly gales. Three hikers found dead on Etive
Mor – two more missing on Ben Nevis; two fishermen washed
off a trawler; a dog, its owner and three policemen washed away
at Blackpool.*

*Got the Christmas tree taken down and the house back to it's
normal trim. Laundry done this morning and hung in front of
the fire as usual – no hope of hanging it outside and hasn't been
for months.*

*We went to visit with W&W and Joan & Murdo – then
down to Aggie Ross's for a lovely lunch of Scotch broth, kosher
turkey and mince pies. Aggie is in her 70s, a lively old gal with
dyed red hair and the spirit of a teenager. She loves to talk and
laugh and sing and give Gaelic lessons. She lives with two cats
in Springwell, a charming Polbain croft house. Aggie and Joan
went to school together.*

# A Matter of Accent

We were sitting by the gleaming fireside in her tidy cottage, Miss
Aggie and I. As always, little plates piled with Scotch pancakes and jam,
oatcakes and cheese and shortbread had been ceremoniously set before
me, and a dainty china teacup balanced precariously on my knee. She
listened closely as I repeated, parrot like, her unfamiliar Gaelic words.

Scots Gaelic is as difficult, obdurate and daunting as the people who invented it. I'm not up to mastering it. But I do want to be able to sing a few favorite Gaelic songs without making my neighbors groan.

Miss Aggie has been teaching the Gaelic to children and adults in the district for more years than anyone could remember. She is a bright old woman with bright red hair, two cats, and a collection of tartan skirts meant for younger legs – she's constantly tugging at her hems. Now retired, the energetic spinster has agreed to help me learn the words to 'Fear A Bhata' and 'Chi Mi Na Morbheanna.' She has worked me through the songs time and again, patiently sounding out the words, correcting my awkward imitations, insisting that I meet her exacting standards for Gaelic pronunciation.

Pronunciation is always an issue in Britain. As one travels northward through rural Lancashire and Cumbria, the English language as we know it is almost lost in a dark forest of tangled tongues and weedy words. North Yorkshire accents are almost impenetrable. And then comes Scotland.

Glaswegians have replaced the letter T with a strangulated glottal stop. They sound as if they're being garrotted in mid word, choking 'Scotland' into 'Sco(!)lun.' Aberdonians use an odd vernacular in which 'where' is pronounced 'far,' and 'what' is replaced by 'fit.' Peerie Shetlanders are as distant from mainland Britain in dialect as they are in nautical miles. Only Edinburgh, like a flat barren field in the midst of a jungle, lacks notable linguistic character; Edinburgh folk are said to mind their pronunciation better than they mind their tongues.

We were surprised, then, to discover in the vast remote Highlands north and west of Inverness a pure, soft, clear and slang free spoken English. Pronunciation is so precise, you can almost envision the way a word is spelled as it is spoken. The word 'squirrel' would be pronounced 'SKWI-rel' here, where I would say 'SKWURL.' In isolated coastal villages like Achiltibuie, English is only a generation away from being a second language, thoughtfully and musically woven by the native Celts into works of conversational art.

It is in Coigach that I have become conscious of my own dialect the lumpish consonants and flat nasal vowels of the American Midwest, over salted with 'yups' and 'you bets.' Peter, our next door neighbor and a concerned parent, brought the problem to my attention. On warm summer days, his three year old son is a regular visitor to Castlehill's kitchen, where Barb plies him with ice cubes. Blond, brown-eyed and infinitely curious, the little boy quickly picked up on my American slang and began using it at home.

His father gently corrected him: "We don't say 'yup,' Christopher. The word is 'yes.'"

"No," said the solemn toddler, "it's 'yup,' actually."

In addition to being a bad influence on children now, I am considered something of a verbal incompetent among adults. The painful discovery came to me on this wintry afternoon at Miss Aggie's, as rain streamed down the windows and a gale buffeting the chimney made the coal fire pulse and glow.

For once I had managed to labor through my two Gaelic party pieces without spraining a tongue or bashing a word, and was feeling rather pleased with myself. Miss Aggie clapped her hands with pleasure, her eyes sparkling. "Oh, that was lovely," she crowed. "Your pronunciation is absolutely perfect! You sound just like a native Highlander!"

Her praise warmed me better than a dram of Glenmorangie, but it hardly prepared me for what she said next.

"There's just one thing I can't understand." She cocked her head with a puzzled frown. "How is it that you can pronounce the Gaelic so well but you can't speak English without that dreadful American accent?"

## January 18th

*I am ensconced in a bed in Ward 8, Raigmore Hospital, Inverness. There are 25 beds in the ward which has brick walls – painted a baby blue. These are surprisingly cheery for buildings that were built during the war as temporary hospitals for servicemen.*

*Somehow I never thought I'd like being in an open ward, but it's really kind of fun. Lots going on and people to talk to and we're all going through the same surgery prep – though my operation will be less serious than many here. Most of us are scheduled for tomorrow. Everyone is in good spirits and friendly, and the staff is attentive and nice. They feed us often – maybe too often, for hospital food is even worse here than in the States. The whole experience is sort of like a big pajama party!*

*There's an old woman in a bed across the way. She's feeling blue, and the nurses assure her that she'll be fine if she just has a nice cup of tea. The other patients stop and sit on her bed and hold her hand and calm her. I have a feeling I won't get much sleep tonight and tomorrow we only get morning tea – then nothing 'til we go down at about 4:00. Long time to wait!*

## January 19th

*Last night the ward was a zoo. There were people running back and forth constantly. A girl was brought in with a hemorrhage about midnight and by the time that was sorted out and things got calmer it was about 4:00 a.m. Breakfast came at 6:00. So no sleep really. The girl is fine now.*

*Seems Evelyn Bolster's sister is in my ward and she and Arthur came to visit this afternoon – it was fun to see them. I went down to the operating theater at 3:00 and was back up before 4:00. It was amazing – they gave me a shot and when I woke up I was in exactly the same place with the same people around – I didn't realize anything had happened! It's much quieter in the ward tonight – everybody who went to the operating theater today is pretty tired. Haven't seen the doctor since but I take it for granted I can leave tomorrow.*

## January 22nd

*Jack came to get me at noon on Thursday and other than feeling a bit groggy I felt just fine and have had no after effects. No worries about payment, either! I feel a bit guilty about taking advantage of a health care system paid for by the British taxpayer – but no one seems to be concerned about it. Here they look at health care as a basic right, rather than a profit center – I'm grateful for that!*

*January 25th*

*I'm sitting here in my kitchen watching the world blow by –
another day of gales and showers. We had thunder and lightning
this morning! It hasn't been cold though – no snow and little frost.
We have rhubarb, chives and daffodils coming up and a few brave
primroses blooming. I feel sorry for the birds – how they can fly
in these winds is beyond me! Since nobody can get outside in this
weather they're starting games and "keep fit" nights down at the
village hall.*

*We're spending many hours sitting by the fireside with guitar
and concertina, making what we like to pretend is music. Anyway,
it beats watching 'Dallas,' which is the current top show on BBC TV
around here. There isn't a day that passes without me thinking how
wonderful it is to not have a TV.*

# Music

Musical talent is a gift from the gods. They owe me.

As a boy I had a lilting soprano voice and the music teacher loved
to show me off to the school. Mrs. Russell played a tune on the piano,
I'd commit it to memory and pretend I was reading the music as I
sang. She pretended so, too, and gave me undeserved good grades
on my report card. Both being Irish, we inoculated my mostly Jewish
classmates with songs like 'Galway Bay' and 'Danny Boy.' Mrs. Russell
was my all-time favorite grade school teacher and I was eager to please
her, but I never succeeded in deciphering those black dots and lines
on the sheet music. And adolescence eventually robbed me of my one
claim to musical competence.

Later, my mother wasted some money on piano lessons for me, and
again I faked reading music for a while. But I hated piano practice and
was never prepared for my lesson. In time, a carefully crafted campaign
of creative sulking freed me from the tyranny of the keyboard. It was
the piano teacher who sulked.

Not that I don't like music. Quite the opposite. I love listening to
music of all kinds. But try as I might, I've never done well at making

music. Through my years I have left a trail of failed enthusiasms: piano, pennywhistle, oboe, harmonica, recorder, even an old bandoneon. Each in turn was abandoned. So when I took that old English concertina down from the shelf in a Glasgow antique/junque shop, Barb's jaw took on that "don't do this" set. Her eyes bored holes in me as I counted out £100 to the dealer. Here we go again.

The pretty little hexagonal instrument has a leather bellows, rosewood sides and pierced, nickel-plated ends. Its 48 metal keys are unmarked, and it came with no instructions. It took some hours, poking keys and hunting for notes, before I was able to play a simple C scale; much longer to locate the sharps and flats that make it fully chromatic. But my 1915 Wheatstone concertina has a rich, mellow tone, and while I haven't learned to play it well and make real music, at least I manage to squeeze out some lovely notes.

Through long quiet evenings in Castlehill, I've sat by the fireside fiddling with the odd little instrument and staring at pages of Scots melodies. It has finally dawned on me that the buttons on its left side correspond with notes on the lines – buttons on the right correspond with the spaces. The concertina has become my Rosetta stone, helping me at last to decipher sheet music! Mrs. Russell would be pleased.

The concertina is more than a diversion. It is a convenient disguise, allowing me to blend in with our growing coterie of Celtic folk musician friends, and share in the drinks that magically appear on the tables before us when we play in Highland pubs. The trick, for me, has been learning to play so quietly that none can hear my fumbled notes. And a difficult trick it is, for while the concertina has a sweet tone, an off-key note can cut through a chord and pierce the heart of a song. But just sitting at a table in the company of good musicians, and clutching a pretty squeezebox, is usually enough to get me by.

There was one day when I even earned a compliment for my playing. Barb and I were exploring the Outer Hebrides with Stookie's Gaelic-speaking girlfriend Mairi. We arrived in South Uist, and a couple of local men were helping us to get settled in an old caravan across the road from her granny's house.

It was a bright day, and I was wearing dark sunglasses – an item seldom needed or even seen in cloudy Uist. After our helpers passed a welcoming bottle (from which they had clearly been partaking), I brought out the concertina and played a few tunes. One of the men turned to the other and said something in Gaelic. I asked Mairi to translate.

She smiled sweetly. "He said you play very well – for a blind man."

## February 24th

*Yesterday was the first nice day in months it seems. Not much sun but no wind. We took a walk down to Badentarbat, stopped to help Donnie fix his car and then went down to the pier where Sheila and Sandy were just coming across from Tanera. We helped them unload and load fish boxes and fish food and stood around nattering for a while. It was so nice to be out and not be blown to bits by the wind. Home for tea – then we stood down by the gate watching the sunset. There was a constant roaring noise and we couldn't figure out what it was – until we realized it was the sound of the sea, which we haven't heard for months because of the constant howling wind!*

*Went into Ullapool for mass, then back to make supper for Pete and Jack. Spent a delightful evening playing music – the time just flies by. Pete brought his dog, Bella, with him – she's really a darling.*

# Bella

Our musician friend Pete Taylor's lovely border collie Bella went with him everywhere. Bella never worked a day in her life with sheep, but she developed something of a reputation as a music critic. When I first played a few notes on my concertina in her presence, she trotted over to me, stared with deep dark eyes and made a few soft moans of distress. Then she placed a dainty paw on my hand, as if to say, "Please don't do that." Then she tried to lick my fingers away from the keys. Finally, she went to the far end of the room and lay down with her paws covering her ears.

Her criticism notwithstanding, I came to love the gentle collie, and looked forward to her visits to Castlehill with Pete. She seemed to enjoy Barb's guitar playing, and anything Pete played on his many musical instruments. She even came, albeit grudgingly, to tolerate my concertina, as long as she was free to leave the room. She was the friendliest of dogs, and the most affectionate, and always, always welcome.

So we were surprised one day when Pete showed up without her. "Where's Bella?"

He threw himself into a chair and passed a hand over his eyes. "She got loose while I was gone. She was seen chasing sheep up at Reiff with another dog. I guess they tore into a ewe and killed it." My heart sank. We all knew the penalty for that.

His voice went flat. "I had to shoot her."

In Coigach, there is a line drawn in blood between sheep and dog. Once it crosses that crimson line, the dog can never be allowed to return.

*March 2nd*

*Sunday we were hit by a terrific gale – quite unexpected. It was one of the worst of the year – knocked the gutters off the Polbain shop and blew the glass out of W&W's greenhouse again. There were whitecaps on even the tiniest lochs and phone cables were down across the road.*

*Monday Jack called the agent in New York who has his manuscript. It was only 3:00 p.m. there but it seems she was already drunk! Jack decided she wouldn't do, at that point – so we're back to square one on selling the novel. It's most discouraging!*

*March 4th*

*Today we went down to Kenny John's in Achduart for tea. He and Ruth gave us a delightful tour of their garden which is full of marvelous trees and bushes – a miniature Inverewe with eucalyptus, rhododendron, camellias etc. – arbors and pools and statues in little hidden glades. The snowdrops, crocus and white heather were blooming. After tea Kenny John brought out his violin and played for us. It was delightful!*

# Party Pieces and Pub Crawls

Kenny John was once the village blacksmith, and even now in his latter years he is a strong man with huge powerful hands. Yet his fingers dance like fairies on the strings of his fiddle and weave gossamer musical magic in the air. One day, after we walked in their lovely garden, Ruth Kenny John brought us in for tea while a cascade of marches and strathspeys, Hebridean airs and lively reels came pouring out of her husband's fiddle to enthrall us. Finally, he closed his performance with a tender old Jacobite tune: 'Will Ye No' Come Back Again?' It was one of his 'party pieces,' and a lovely way to bring our visit to an end.

Coigach being not that long removed from a time before radios and TVs and electronic gadgets took on the task of home entertainment, people here are good at the task themselves. And while Kenny John Macleod is certainly one of the best, many here have songs to sing and stories to tell and musical instruments close in reach when visitors come to call.

Everyone has his own signature contribution to the festivities – his party piece. And even though his may be a song known to all others at a ceilidh – perhaps even known around the world – courtesy gives him a certain degree of ownership on that particular evening. When Anne Irish is there, she'll be called on to sing 'The Black Velvet Band', for it is acknowledged to be her party piece. Her father-in-law John Alec is a fine Gaelic singer whose 'Fear A Bhata' is always in demand. Donnie Darling is noted for singing 'North To Alaska' in pub and ceilidh, and though he seldom gets beyond the first verse, no one else would presume to start it before him.

Party pieces become so linked to individuals that the sound of a few notes or words can call them to mind. I can't hear 'Big John Maclean' without thinking of Jimmy. 'Dead Skunk In The Middle Of The Road' is Caroline's. 'Bonny At Morn' belongs to Tommy and Heather, and 'Without My Walkin' Stick' never sounds right without Dik Banovich and his jazz guitar.

It doesn't even have to be music. The first year in Coigach, lacking both instrument and singing voice, my party piece was recitation from memory: 'The Cremation of Sam McGee.' It was often called for, and I like to think my northern American accent – sounding close to Canadian – helped listeners hear the howl of the wind, feel the chill of the Arctic night in Robert Service's Yukon Gold Rush ballad.

Once I got to where I could find most of the buttons on my concertina most of the time, I learned to play 'Da Old Resting Chair', a nostalgic slow air by legendary Shetland fiddler Tom Anderson. Barb's guitar accompaniment covered the worst of my mistakes, and my friends were kind enough to ask for it more reliably than I played it.

The nature of ceilidhs and pub music sessions is such that strangers, newcomers, beginners, learners, shy people, children, passing drunks and even total incompetents are encouraged, cajoled and supported in any effort they make to entertain. These are the most generous audiences on earth, for they are constantly giving to each other.

Barb and I have fallen in love with the British tradition of pub sessions – impromptu music that springs up whenever people bring instruments into a pub. The music is mostly traditional – Scottish, Irish and English songs, airs, jigs and reels – but songs from the Continent and across the Atlantic come into it as well, and the North Sea oil boom has injected Country & Western into the mix. Any music that's fun to sing or play is fair game, and far better to listen to than the bong-bong of the fruit machines that infect so many pubs now.

We have followed our musical friends into pubs across the length and breadth of Scotland and even down into Lancashire. There's a sense of anticipation as we crowd into a corner of the bar and order the first round of drinks. Someone pulls a guitar from its case and starts to tune it – another draws a pennywhistle from his pocket to provide an E for tuning. A fiddle comes out, or a mandolin, and for a while there is subdued cacophony as each musician essays a few riffs on his instrument. Gradually the notes coalesce into a recognizable tune, and the music begins.

Some patrons turn to watch the fun. Many will later join in the songs, or go to fetch their own instruments. Others simply nurse their drinks, and listen or not, as they wish. The publican beams, for music means the prospect of happy patrons and more drinking and perhaps a profitable after-hours session. He'll likely send the music-makers a round of drinks to keep them going past closing time. And other bar patrons may do the same.

This spring, we've played group sessions at the hotel pub up in tiny Drumbeg, where genial publican Mackay brings out his bagpipes after the door is locked and adds to the fun. And at pubs in Portmahomack, Tain, Ullapool and Dingwall. When the Highland Games were on in Skye, we were all invited down to stay the weekend at a hostel in Uig, where we played for our bed and breakfast. For a couple of not particularly musical Americans, this itinerant musical life is an adventure and a delight, and we just hope no critic listens too closely and ejects us from it!

With all these weekend peregrinations, I have been missing a few of my traditional Saturday outings with Murdo. Fortunately, others in Coigach have volunteered to get him out to the Fuaran when I'm gone, so he won't be missing the company of his old friends.

## March 17th

*The pace of life is beginning to pick up – hotels and restaurants etc. are opening for the Easter tourist trade and more and more people are coming into the community. Days are longer and busy – lots of building and remodeling going on. Even with the terrible weather we've been busy – it's snowing like mad outside right now, and gale winds are whipping at the daffodils. This is great country for developing patience, tolerance, character and mildew. We just keep staring at the calendar and reminding each other that sooner or later summer must come. Mustn't it?*

## March 24th

*The chimney sweeps came today. They travel around from village to village and clean chimneys – do a good job too. They sure got a load out of ours – it hasn't been cleaned since we came and burning coal builds up a lot of soot, so we were glad to see them. Evelyn came with her violin again this afternoon. We need a few more practice sessions!*

Barb is in the sitting room with Evelyn Bolster, rehearsing for their debut on Tuesday night. The local women's guild is having its last meeting of the winter, a tea thing, and Barb and Evelyn will be playing a group of guitar/fiddle duets – mostly Scottish country dance tunes, with a few Irish songs thrown in. I've been hiding in my office this morning to keep them from being self-conscious.

The Easter holiday is almost upon us, and our pub is beginning to fill up with bonglies. We're still getting snow and hail squalls, but there are already bicyclists camping on the beach at Achnahaird, and a bunch of guys with kayaks! Next week the pub at the Summer Isles Hotel will be open again, a great milestone in the social year up here. We're just a month away from the beginning of lambing, and then we'll be into the clipping time again. It's all passing too quickly.

The gals are beginning to sound pretty good out there.

# Spring

*April 4th*

*The Summer Isles pub is open again and we had a great night there Saturday – a nice mix of local people. The Fuaran was impossible – full of strangers and smoke, though we should have about a month respite before the bonglie season starts up for real. We ended up at Leslie's and had a good sing-song. Ken the Bread is back and stopped in for a visit the other day, after a good winter in Australia.*

*Jack's out with Alasdair West and the Manager to try getting the sheep off Mullagrach. I don't know if the seas will allow it – it will be tricky!*

*Yesterday there was a big tour bus from Düsseldorf parked in Polbain with its passengers walking around snapping pictures. Donnie Darling isn't too happy about seeing Germans on the road below his house – seems it brings back memories of his service during World War II. "The king paid me a shilling a day to shoot the buggers."*

## Connections

It was a Saturday, and as usual I was at the Fuaran with Murdo, Alasdair West and John Alec. As usual, rain beat against the windows. As usual that early in the day, the pub was not yet busy and the four of us were gathered at the bar. The comfortable, predictable conversation rambled from sheep and weather and people to times the older men had shared. Quiet conversation, except for John Alec whose booming voice betrayed the gradual onset of his deafness. Quiet conversation was shattered by the jangle of the phone behind the bar.

Andy quickly set down the glass he was polishing and picked up the receiver. "F-fuaran." He glanced at me. "Yes, he's here." He handed the phone across the bar to me. "It's for you, Jack."

I was mystified. I had never taken a call at the Fuaran before, nor have I since. Who would be calling me here? "Hello?"

The connection wasn't good, but the voice was familiar. And American. "Hi Jack – it's Perry. How's it going?"

Perry? Perry was a film producer in Minneapolis. We had worked together on projects in the past, most recently on a documentary in West Africa – but even that was five years ago, and we hadn't been in contact since. "Perry? Where are you?"

"London. I'm here for a couple of days and I'm free for the weekend. I thought I might come up for a day and see you!"

Come up for a day. "Uh, Perry – do you have any idea how far this is from London?" Americans aren't noted for their sense of geography, but this was ridiculous. "It would take you at least a full day just to get here, and another to get back – you'd have to blow at least three days just to say 'hello.'"

"Oh. I didn't know." Disappointed silence. "Where are you, exactly?" I told him. "Scotland? No kidding?" He hadn't a clue.

"How the hell did you find me here?"

"Well, I knew you were somewhere near Ullapool, wherever that is. So I called the operator there."

"The operator in Ullapool knew I was at the Fuaran?!"

As Perry explained it, she didn't. But she knew there was an American living somewhere in Coigach. I wasn't listed in the phone book, so she called Hectoria, the postmistress in Achiltibuie. Hecky gave her the number for Castlehill, but no one answered there. Undeterred, the Ullapool operator rang the post office again. Hecky must have looked at the calendar and checked the clock on the wall. "Och, it's Saturday – he'll be at the Fuaran with Murdo."

Perry and I never did manage to get together. But at least he knew that I had connections somewhere in Scotland.

*April 7th*

*Today was another beautiful day of blue skies and sun. Yesterday was too – we spent the morning walking and visiting. All the lochs were like mirrors reflecting the blue sky, fluffy clouds and white mountain peaks. Saw a herd of eight red deer – stags and hinds trotting along near the road – a beautiful sight!*

*Jack helped the Manager with dipping and jagging and dosing 700 sheep at Blairbuie. He was quite impressed with the dipper and the way it all was handled – says that the Manager really seems to know his business.*

# The Summer Isles

The Summer Isles Hotel in Achiltibuie is owned by an imperious Englishman who has shown little fondness for the locals. For six days a week, many locals reciprocate by shunning the hotel and its pub. I can well understand their feelings, for this was the place that had refused us as 'transients' the first time we came to Coigach.

So Monday through Saturday, the Summer Isles pub is a pretty quiet place. But even Highlanders can't hold a grudge where whisky is at stake. The owners of the Fuaran observe the Free Church ban on Sunday commerce, while the aforementioned Englishman has no such Sabbatarian scruples. So the pub attached to the Summer Isles does a booming business on Sundays.

It's a small and spartan room, this pub, just a short bar with a few stools, and two hard wooden benches against the walls. Plain white painted wainscoting lines the walls. Outside, a shaded veranda overlooking Loch Broom takes the overflow on holiday weekends when the pub becomes standing-room-only. On summer Sunday afternoons, the Summer Isles pub is packed with revelers. Young mothers gather on the veranda nattering with friends, enjoying a smoke and a pint while watching their kiddies race and chase in the sunlit driveway below. By the time you get your dram from the bar and dodge, squeeze, push and elbow your way to the outer edge of the milling crowd, whatever of your whisky you haven't spilled might well have evaporated. No matter, you can always turn back and push in again – just being there is all that counts.

One Sunday I drove old Murdo there in our little sedan. He enjoyed riding, for he had never in his life driven a car. We came early, to ensure a seat for him on the high-backed wooden bench inside the door. West was there too, and John Alec, and they were able to have a fine conversation for a few minutes before half the population of Coigach crowded in around us. In the hour that followed, many a pint and dram passed back from the bar, and more than a few were drained in our corner before Murdo and I decided to go back home for tea with Joan and Barb.

I took the old man by the elbow and steadied him down the steep driveway to where my car was parked. To be honest, I wasn't all that steady myself. But I propped him against the fender, opened the car door and helped him to clamber in. I was pleased with myself for remembering, despite the alcoholic haze, to fasten the unfamiliar seat belt for him before navigating around to get in on the other side. Very deliberately I pulled the door closed and latched my own seat belt. One can't be too safe, you know.

The two of us sat there in the car, ready to go except for one puzzling thing. Murdo sat to my right, staring blankly at the steering wheel mysteriously placed in front of him. I sat befuddled with an ignition key in my hand and nowhere to insert it. Outside the car, knowing bystanders grinned at us. Wordlessly, with the silent, studied movements of sleepwalkers, we got out of the car and changed places. And with great dignity, looking neither right nor left, we drove slowly out of the Summer Isles car park and crept carefully back to Polbain.

## April 11th

*Easter Sunday. W&W came over for breakfast. I had made hot cross buns for Easter and we had a lovely morning feast. Main topic of conversation – the scene put on by 'the Poet' in the Fuaran Friday night!*

# The Poet

Here's how Wee Les came to be called 'the Poet.' As you would expect, Wee Les is not a large man. He is an incomer, a bearded Bohemian type who lives in the council houses and blinks out at the world through thick steel-rimmed glasses. When he isn't mending prawn creels or working on someone's fishing boat, Wee Les is a self-styled poet, author, photographer, naturalist, whatever – a creative soul, a dreamer of big dreams. In conversation at the pub, he weaves airy schemes for making money with one or another of his various talents – none of which ever quite materializes.

This one time, Wee Les hit on the notion to organize a program of poetry and music at the Fuaran. He even distributed hand-made posters around the community to announce the event. It was Easter week, and the first tourists of the year were swarming in Coigach, so the pub that night was packed. The music was a great success – a fiddler, guitarist and Pete Taylor – and the ale and whisky were flowing. By the time Wee Les stood up to read his poetry the place was in full swing and full of holiday talk. Over the uproar, one could see him mouthing words, but few if any were heard. His free verse made no more impact on the surrounding cacophony than arrows launched into a fog.

The Poet retreated from the field to slake his thirst while even more people elbowed their way into the pub. Then, undeterred, he ventured a second reading. It was getting close to last call for drinks, the air was heavy with smoke and the crowd joyfully lubricated. Even nose to nose, people had to shout to be heard. Which they did. Art, Culture and Personal Improvement were clearly the last things on anyone's mind.

Nothing daunted, Wee Les launched into his introduction. Two people stood directly in front of him in animated conversation. He flapped his poetry papers. No one seemed to notice. He stood on tiptoe and raised his voice. No one seemed to hear. He tried again, cupping his ear in a vain attempt to hear his own words in the tornado of sound around him. The wall of drinkers, smoke and noise was impenetrable.

When all else failed, he drew himself up like a rooster at dawn and let out a high-pitched yell. "Shut up! I'd appreciate it!" His words struck the room like a lightning bolt. The crowd went absolutely silent. "There's more to life," the poet declaimed, "than booze and cigarettes!"

Everyone stood there with a drink in one hand and a fag in the other, looking vaguely puzzled by this novel idea. The silence lasted for as long as it took the angry, diminutive poet to push his way out the door. Then someone said," Oh well – every village needs one." The others took pensive drags on their smokes, raised their glasses and turned back to their conversations.

## April 18th

*We have hundreds of bright yellow daffodils in front of Castlehill now, and the yard is a delight to the eye. The weather has shifted from spring to winter and again to spring and again and again... but spring is getting the upper hand, bit by bit. The ewes are heavy with lamb now, and the first little ones are expected in three weeks, at the beginning of May.*

Easter week was the official beginning of the tourist season, and our isolated, snug little world is turning upside down. Last Friday night the pub was crammed with unfamiliar voices, faces, noises; yesterday we almost got wiped out on the single-track road to Ullapool because I was still rounding the corners at the hellish speed I got used to when the roads were winter-empty. Now it takes considerably longer to drive anywhere because of all the stopping and backing-up necessary on a heavily-used single-track road.

Having grown up in an urban world where every day was filled with unfamiliar faces, most of the people I saw on the streets, in stores, in offices, even in my neighborhood were strangers. Here we know everyone, and strangers are – well – strange. I can meet a car on the road 15 miles from home and know at once if it's a neighbor, or an outsider. The local people refer to outsiders as 'strangers', and the word has a deeply literal meaning for them. And now for us as well.

# Lambing

Alasdair West fell down in the Fuaran and broke his ankle. That was bad enough, but West himself hastened to cite a further indignity: "I'd just come in the door. I hadn't even had a drink!" I think this pained him as much as the injury itself. It was his brand-new pair of tackety boots that brought him down. The boots had stiff soles with shiny metal tacks – good for clambering on the rocks of Coigach, once they're roughed up a bit. But new and smooth, they skittered like ice skates on the pub's tile floor and hastened his literal downfall.

It could not have happened at a worse time: early May, and the beginning of the lambing season. West had already gathered his sheep in from the common grazing, into the fenced park where the ewes would give birth under his watchful eye.

Why watchful? Because in the eons since sheep were domesticated, they have become less than perfect mothers. Some need help to give birth, some refuse to feed their lambs, some drop twins but only have milk for one, some die in birth and leave orphaned lambs behind. The shepherd's lot, at lambing time, is to be a veterinary gynecologist and pediatrician, patrolling the steep hills of the park at dawn and dusk, in all weathers, seven days a week throughout the month of May. It is the most demanding time in the shepherd's year. And Alasdair West was unable to walk.

Angus was away at university, Davy working in the city, leaving Ali the only able-bodied West in Achnahaird. Ali had been a merchant seaman, then a fisherman, and now had a full-time job as Coigach's postman. At this time in his life, he was not overfond of sheep, or shepherding, or working too closely under his father's critical eye. However, Nature doesn't concern herself with our preferences and job schedules. The lambs were coming, ready or not.

I offered to help. Not that I knew anything about lambing. But I could make myself useful by walking part of the park, locating ewes and lambs with problems, calling Ali over to help, and perhaps learning to do some of the work myself. Alasdair seemed glad of the offer, and so I became an apprentice at the lambing.

Every morning that month I got up in the dark, dressed, pulled on my wellies and drove around to Achnahaird. The light would be on in West's kitchen. The room was small, warm and crowded, with a drying rack for wet clothes suspended by rope and pulley from the ceiling to catch the heat of the stove. The men would be at the table already, Alasdair giving unneeded directions as strong-minded fathers will, Ali taking it in with a grain of salt as strong-minded sons do. Margaret, brisk and cheerful, bustled about making sure everyone had plenty of tea. As the first signs of morning showed over the eastern hills, Ali and I emptied our steaming mugs and set out for the park.

Lambing mornings are always chill, sometimes wet, and you can't help feeling a shiver of anticipation, looking up at the black bulk of the hill against the lightening sky. Up there new life was happening, and we had a role to play. We climbed the fence and split up, each taking half the park, looking for new lambs or ewes having difficulties.

In the first days there were few lambs. Most of the ewes grazed quietly or lay dozing in the heather, their sides swollen with promise. Here and there, a skinny white bundle on pipe-cleaner legs stood bent-kneed beneath its mother, demanding sustenance. Tramping over uneven ground that always seemed uphill, I often stopped to catch my breath and take in the unfolding scenery. The slanting light of early morning left voluptuous shadows on the mountainsides. Winds are usually at their lowest at this time of day, and in these spaces even silence has a ring to it.

I listened for sounds of distress, looked for ewes on their sides with legs stretching in the agony of birth, lambs down or abandoned. At first, when I found a problem, I'd hasten over to Ali's side of the park for help. Patiently he taught me, showed me how to draw a lamb from the womb, and wipe residue from the afterbirth on the ewe's muzzle to give her the scent and taste of her newborn.

You've heard a thousand times about the "miracle of birth." Try watching a newborn lamb struggle to its feet, feel its way around the underside of its mother and home in on the source of that life-giving milk, before you tell me it's a cliche. This alone was ample reward for getting up on lambing mornings.

We brought orphaned lambs down from the park, to be put onto ewes that had lost their own. Nature dictates that a ewe will give milk only to her own lamb, and refuse it to others. There are aerosol sprays supposed to fool ewes into accepting orphans, but the traditional lamb-skin vest worked as well or better to give the orphan a scent she would accept as her own.

Occasionally, the maternal instincts didn't kick in for ewes giving birth for the first time. Sometimes a ewe might refuse to nurse her own lamb, and require a little on-the-job training. Barb did a drawing of the Manager giving such a lesson that same season.

Ali and I walked the park morning and evening, rain or shine, seven days a week until the last lamb was born late in May. After the dawn patrol, we'd go back to report to Alasdair while Margaret served up a hearty breakfast; then Ali would rush off to his work at the post office.

As the lambing season progressed, Ali grew in confidence and knowledge. Early morning sessions between father and son evolved from lectures to conferences, as Ali became Alasdair's surrogate in the field. I don't know if Ali could see the growing pride in his father's eyes, but he must have felt it. And I think he began to enjoy working with sheep for the first time.

Now comes a delicate point. Men and sheep. And intimacy. Ahem. No, this isn't about ancient jokes and 'the ugliest one in the flock.' It's about the complex relationship between man and animal when their lives are involved in each other, and in many ways depend on each other.

Let me begin by saying that except for the littlest lambs, I do not find sheep loveable, or even likeable. The adult North Country Cheviot has baleful cat's eyes. It is self-destructively stupid. It is evasive and sly, greedy, stubborn, uncooperative, and remarkably vulnerable. It is a mobile food processor with vegetation constantly going in at one end and turds marching out the other. When new spring grass gives it raging diarrhoea, its woolly backside is disgusting beyond belief.

Yet whenever they work together, sheep men talk to their sheep. With affection and anger, soothingly, bitterly, they speak as if the dumb creatures could understand. Or care. Listen to a weather-worn, hill-hardened crofter as he draws a lamb from the womb, and inevitably he'll be murmuring "easy, lassie" and "you're almost done, girl" as he tries to calm the ewe with a gentle voice. Watch him struggle to control a wild hill sheep fighting to escape his shears, and you'll get a lesson in colorful cursing. The communication is only one-way, but it is intensely intimate.

How so? Consider that the crofter has known each sheep from its birth, seen it shed its placenta, struggle to its feet and seek its mother's teat. If it was an orphan, he may have wrapped it in his own jacket to shelter it from rain, and brought it home to be warmed by the kitchen stove and bottle-fed. If it became ill, as many do, he may have nursed it back to health. He has handled it time and again for medication, castration, tail docking, sorting, dipping and clipping. His clothes and boots and arms have been stained with its shit, his fingers have probed beneath its fleece, his blades have traced the contours of its body, he knows its smell and has felt the beat of its heart.

When you or I see a flock of sheep, they are just sheep in the aggregate, one much like the next. To the crofter, they are individuals who have consumed much of his life. He knows which ones are hardy and which are weak, which are good mothers and which are not, which to select for another year's breeding and which to send off to market. He has power of life and death over them, and is called to exercise it every year. So there is both a softness and a hardness in the relationship between man and sheep, as there is in the landscape of Coigach.

## *May 14th*

*Unfortunately, Jack's book was rejected by another agent so he's starting on a revision. I think we're going to have to accept the idea of going back to the States for a while.*

*Lambing is going beautifully for the most part. It was interesting working with the Manager. He has an efficient fank set up at Blairbuie. Jack held the lambs and I handed Kenny the tools to operate on them, poor things!.*

# A Lousy Day to be a Lamb

There is nothing so joyful as watching lambs in the spring. They are soft then, and snowy white, and sweetly trusting and playful. The young ones quickly band up into play groups and invent games you'll easily recognize: tag, follow-the-leader, king of the hill. There's no mistaking the rules – exactly the same as in your own childhood. The lambs leap and run and sniff and taste and explore every new thing in a world of new things.

Ewes keep one wary eye on their babies as they graze. Should anything appear to threaten their safety, a loud maternal "ba-a-a" brings the leggy little fluff balls racing to their mothers' sides. Feeding times are unmistakable. The lamb tucks its head under its mother's flank, and butts her udder aggressively to let down her milk. Afterward, the ewe might lie down on the sunlit grass, with her sleeping lamb curled warm and safe between her legs.

It is an idyllic scene, but it belies the trauma of a new lamb's early life. For sooner or later comes the day of horrors.

It begins with big men and frightful dogs coming over the home hill. Suddenly the world is dangerous. Instinctively, lamb and ewe press into the protective flock and follow it blindly. When it stops, they discover themselves trapped in a pen. A man comes through the gate holding a long stick with a metal hook on the end. As the lamb tries to scurry behind its mother, he feels the hook clutching his hind leg, and he is pulled backward, grabbed by the scruff, and hoisted up away from the flock. He is surrounded by people. It is the first time since birth he has been separated from the flock, and he is confused and frightened.

Someone pinches up the flesh behind the lamb's shoulders and jabs him with a needle. At the fleeting pressure of the injection, he bleats. His mother answers from somewhere far away – but he can no longer see her. He struggles, but a man is holding him by the shoulders and his back is pressed against a fence. There is worse to come.

One of the men grabs the lamb's tail and jerks it hard. The shock masks pain as the man twists the end of the tail off! He tosses it into a bucket. There are two buckets for these tail remnants – one for ewe lambs, one for males, to be tallied later. A Highland calculator.

Now the lamb's head is locked in the man's grasp. Wielding a steel tool that looks like a ticket punch, he crimps down on the edge of its ear. Snip, snip – bits of the ear go flying. The notched ear pattern, called a 'lug mark,' is unique to each crofter. It will help him identify his lambs when they are mixed in with Coigach flocks on the common grazing.

Next, for the little males, comes the ring. A small bright blue rubber ring stretched in a pliers-like device. The man slips the ring over the lamb's scrotum and releases it from the tool. The ring snaps tight, cutting off circulation to the little one's testicles. In a week or so, the scrotum will fall off and the lamb will officially become a wether – a castrated male.

A 'buist' may be smeared on the lamb's shoulder, hip, head or back. Buists are red or blue paint marks crofters use to identify their sheep. Think color coding. Each crofter has his own coded combination of buist color and location to help him quickly separate his own from others on the common grazing, or sort which are to be kept from those bound for market.

Finally, the person holding the lamb dunks it into a tub of stinking chemicals, then releases it into the pen. Ears, tail and testicles aching, eyes burning from the dip, the dazed lamb staggers, bleats, seeks out his mother for comfort. He will never have a worse day – until his last one.

Some of the orphan lambs lead a privileged life. Oh, they too have to suffer that one horrid day, but then – if they're lucky – they get adopted by children in the village. Our next door neighbor's little boy, Christopher, has four at the moment.

## May 17th

*Sally Drake has four lambs that she's raising and I was lamb-sitting for her today. Jack and I went over and fed them twice – each holding two bottles. There are two little ewes and two wethers – the biggest one Christopher named "Little Jack" (he now calls Jack "Big Jack). One ewe is a real piggy – finishes her bottle and then tries to find milk under Little Jack and gets peed on for her pains. The other little ewe is just new and still a bit shy and teeny. Jamie, the other wether, was a bit shaky for a while and they thought he might die.*

*But he seems better now. They're so cute and get all excited when they see us and know they're to be fed.*

Christopher is very attached to his charges, especially Little Jack. But emotional attachments cut both ways. When Sally decided that a lambskin rug in her bedroom needed cleaning, she tossed it in their front-loading washing machine. Christopher toddled into the kitchen, looked in the machine's window, saw the fleece sloshing round and round, and began to bawl: "Oh, no! Little Jack!"

The little ones – sheep as well as humans – recover quickly from the traumas of youth. Unfortunately, the lambs grow up to be sheep. Fortunately, Christopher has better prospects.

# Summer

## June 17th

*Woke up this morning to news that the Arcadia, a trawler from Lossiemouth out of Lochinver, was found wrecked on the rocks near Stoer Point. All five crew were drowned – they were diving for bodies all day. No one knows why it happened – the weather was good at the time she went down. Jack played pool with a fellow who'd been out on her earlier in the week – spent the day seeing what it was like to be on a trawler. Another boat went down there in the same spot in 1976 also with five crew. There was a rumor that an Arcadia crewman's wife had lost her first husband in that '76 disaster – I don't know whether that's true – I hope not.*

## My Own Blades

In my first summer of clipping, I was loaned whichever set of blade shears no one else was using. Naturally enough, these weren't exactly the finest tools in Coigach, and I quickly developed the blisters to prove it.

Most of the blade shears I used were old, some rusty, few well sharpened. Dull blades make the clipping harder. When clipping a dirty, matted or sandy fleece, they tend to separate. Alasdair spent some time teaching me how to cross one blade over the other and sharpen them on a flat stone.

The design of blade shears goes back thousands of years to the Bronze Age. The shears we use in Coigach would be easily recognized

by the ancient Greeks and Romans. Unlike scissors, which pivot on a more or less central pin, blade shears are sprung at the back. They are closed by a squeeze of the hand, and spring open when released. Each pair has its own feel, depending on the strength of the spring and the set of the blades. You can almost tell how well they are cutting by the sound when the blades click together.

With my second season of clipping fast approaching, I determined to find my own blade shears. It wasn't as easy as I thought. The single-bowed blades I found in Dingwall shops felt spongy. All of the double-bowed blades in Inverness seemed weak. I tried adjustable blades in North Yorkshire, to no avail. There was considerable variation in feel, even among identical models, but none of them felt or sounded quite right.

Finally, in June, Barb and I went to the Royal Highland Show in Edinburgh and stopped in the display tent of Burgon & Ball, the world's largest maker of sheep shears. And there, on the wall, I found my shears.

They had a nice heft to them, fit my hand perfectly, felt smooth and sharp and good. The two blades were joined by a C-shaped spring at the back, giving a nice firm action. And when I squeezed them, the steel edges sang sweetly against each other and closed with a ringing snap. They were a perfect instrument, a veritable Stradivarius of sheep shears. If an inanimate object could speak, these blades would have said "take me, I'm yours!"

But the factory sales rep who ran the tent had other ideas. "I'm sorry, sir, but those are the only in-curved blades I have. I cannot sell them – I need them for display." He was cool and crisp, in a pin-striped suit. "Would you like me to have a set sent out from the factory?"

I was crestfallen. I wanted them now. "Well, could you send me this particular one?"

"I can't be certain, sir. But they will certainly be the same model."

"No – this is the one I want."

"I'm sorry sir. Perhaps if you can come back tomorrow when the show closes..."

"We'll be gone before then."

"I'm sorry, sir."

Disappointed, we left the tent and wandered through the grounds, past agricultural displays, livestock pens, pipe bands and Highland games. We watched a sheep shearing competition – it was all done by pro's using machines, of course – but Barb studied the action of the fleece-rollers as they bundled and tied the wool, and picked up some techniques which would prove useful back at Achnahaird.

I was still sulking about the shears as we made our way back toward the car park. Just as we were approaching the Burgon & Ball exhibit, the man I had talked to emerged from the tent and strode away toward a tea vendor down the row. If at first you don't succeed... "Wait here a minute, Barb." I ducked into the tent.

A pleasant young man was holding the fort during his boss's tea break. "May I help you, sir?"

"Yes. I'd like to buy those shears."

"Certainly, sir." He took the blades – my blades – down from the display. "Will there be anything else, sir?"

"No, thank you." I felt a bubble rising in my chest. "That will be quite enough." Nervously eyeing the tent entrance, I whipped out my wallet and paid for the blades.

"Shall I wrap them for you, sir?"

"No, thank you." I glanced at my watch. "I'm in a bit of a hurry."

"Let me put them into a bag, at least."

"Yes, yes. Whatever." How long does it take a man to get a cup of tea?

"Thank you very much, sir." He handed me my purchase. "I'm sure you'll be pleased."

"I am already," I said with a quick smile. "And thank you!" Snatching the bag, I hastened out of the tent – and almost collided with the Burgon & Ball representative coming back with his cup of tea. "Oops! Sorry!" My apology was over-the-shoulder as I bustled Barb off toward the car park. The man stared after us, probably wondering where he'd seen me before. He'd soon remember, once he saw his depleted shear display.

Too bad about that nice young clerk, though.

## June 22nd

*We went back to the fair to watch the machine shearing competitions. Ian Mowat (the contract shearer at Inverpolly last year) got into the semi-finals but I don't know how he did finally because we had to leave to get to Inverness to do some shopping.*

*Bill stopped in after we got home and we went to the pub for a little pool. Donnie was there – resplendent in his new false teeth. Makes him look ten years younger! He also said he'd heard another rumor that we were buying Castlehill. I wish it were true.*

# Change

If we were to bring home a crowd of screaming naked cannibals in America, our neighbors would ask, "What in hell are those savages doing in your house?"

Here in Coigach, they'd more likely say, "someone at the shop was asking, would you be needing anything special in the way of groceries?"

So it's not surprising that the question of our intentions toward Castlehill has been broached so indirectly. Joan herself had touched on it a year earlier with "someone at the store asked..."

Could we buy Castlehill? Not with the dwindling resources we have. Would we if we could? We don't know. The fact is, we don't know what we're going to do.

We have been living for two years on the proceeds of selling our house in Minneapolis. I had hoped that somehow I could wring a living out of writing fiction, but so far my efforts have only produced postage bills and rejection letters. Soon we will run out of money.

I am not worried. Yet. Over tea in the kitchen, Barb and I have long, quiet conversations about hopes and possibilities and prospects. I have been able to make a living by freelance script writing for many years. I am optimistic. But that was in the city, among producers, longtime clients and friends. Barb is realistic .

What about a transatlantic future? Make money there, a home here? The dream of buying and settling in to Castlehill is alluring, but we're not even sure that's what we want for the rest of our lives. The pull of our families, our oldest friends, our own country is hard to resist.

So we're going back to America at the end of September. For a while, at least.

Now, as our departure is on the horizon, Joan and Murdo are dropping hints, ever so subtly, that Castlehill could easily be ours. No direct discussion, of course – that wouldn't be Coigach.

Murdo has tested the waters several times during our Saturday outings, complaining about the bother of keeping two houses, heaving deep sighs about not being able to see his old friends once I'm gone back to America. The times we've spent together in the Fuaran and the Summer Isles have re-connected him to life in the community, and he's loth to see an end to it.

I'm feeling the impending loss as well. Whether he and Joan have become surrogate parents – or Barb and I surrogate children – we have grown together these past two years and the thought of separation now is hard. We hope to be able to come back next year – brightly say we will be back – but who can say, for sure?

In recent weeks, while Joan tends to the tea, Murdo has dwelt on Coigach ways and people and events as if he feared they'd soon be lost to memory. He tells us that his great grandfather came from Isle Ristol, just off Old Dornie harbor. Once there was a settlement of perhaps twelve houses, and his great grandmother ran a pub. When the tenants were evicted, they moved to Tanera and the houses on Isle Ristol were pulled down to make dikes. Not a trace remains.

*Murdo and Donnie were telling us about taking cattle off the islands years ago, where they used to be put over winter to fatten on good grass near the water. What a horrendous job! They would get wild being out there for months on their own, and would have to be lassoed and their feet tied together – then rolled into the boat – first a dinghy and then the big boat.*

*Murdo recalled a particularly wild and unmanageable bunch he'd taken off when he was the Tanera boatman. When he'd gotten them into the fank here, he had to call a heavy lorry from Inverness to come and take them to market in Dingwall. When the driver asked why they still had ropes around their legs, Murdo told him it was a ploy to get more money for them – he would charge for the rope too!*

*Yesterday Murdo told another story about taking horses on and off the islands. He said a man who owned horses that were hired out to do plowing was cruel – he starved and mistreated them. When Tanera needed plowing done, the horses would be put into Murdo's boat and taken across. He said horses always stood on the windward side – unlike sheep or cows who always went to leeward and threatened to swamp the boat if there was a wind.*

*Although worked hard, for they cost money to hire, the plow horses were very well treated on Tanera – fed and pampered as never they were by their owner. Murdo said there was one horse – a lovely white one – who, whenever he saw the Tanera boat coming across to Badentarbat, would run down and jump in by himself, eager for a working holiday on the island!*

Murdo speaks of the old days when people would gather of an evening and tell stories and sing. He says there was a custom where five or six men would be sitting before the fire and the man at one end would light a pipe and pass it along and each would take a puff until it was gone. Then the next man would do the same with his pipe and so they would share the smoke as they told their stories.

The world he and Joan were born into was small, communal, familial. The stories of old men were little different from those of the young, for change was slow and the outside world was far away and friends stayed where they belonged. Now people cross oceans in less time than it once took to go to Dingwall market. It is a lot for an old man to bear.

## July 6th

*Sunday we celebrated the 4th of July – put up our flag – everyone loves that! When we went into the Summer Isles there was a big crowd and an air of expectation. This year we bought a round of 50 whiskies – one for each state – and passed them to all and sundry. At closing we went to Ken's caravan for a wee ceilidh, came back here for dinner and went to the pub for a while – then back here for our own Independence Day ceilidh.*

*Willie John was in great form doing imitations (especially of Jimmy Mackay), Pete and a friend sang duets and we put out sandwiches for a packed house. Jack Thomson turned up in a ten-gallon hat and cowboy boots, and a star on his Western shirt that said "Deputy." When I asked him "why deputy?" he said he couldn't remember how to spell "sheriff."*

*When we finally tried to turn in about 3:30 am we found Big Leslie and her boys asleep in our bed! No problem, we slept in our guest bed. It was a wonderful day and a good bash. Monday we had breakfast and took Leslie and the kids home, Anne Irish came for a while at lunch and we took a walk down to the harbor.*

# Counterfeit Highlanders

Because it is remote, traditional, and one of the few remaining areas in Scotland where Gaelic survives, Coigach is something of a cultural curiosity, attracting all sorts of people eager to see the 'real' Highlands. Folk musicians search here for the roots of their Celtic music. Most tourists come looking for mountains and sea and unaccustomed space, or to savor an imaginary past conjured up by 'Rob Roy' and 'Brigadoon.' Some come as they would to a zoo, expecting to be entertained and shown exotic species – examined from a safe distance, of course. And because all of these visitors bring money into Coigach every summer, it is important to meet their expectations.

So when the Ceilidh Place hotel in Ullapool asked our musician friend Pete Taylor to entertain a visiting group of American travel writers, and he invited us to come along, I was reluctant. "I don't want to disappoint anyone. They're not coming all the way up here to see more Americans." When Pete protested that he needed accompaniment, I pointed out that while Barb could back him on her guitar, my singing was doubtful at best. And my concertina skills could barely meet the challenge of 'Twinkle, Twinkle Little Star.'

Pete laughed. "True – but you don't have to do much – just play a few chords and sing along on the choruses. C'mon, I need your support."

"But our Minnesota accents..."

"So? I have an English accent. But these are Americans – they won't know the difference. And they'll probably have a few drinks before we play. The Tourist Board billed this as a Highland ceilidh night, and they'll assume we're the real thing. Besides, I can't get anyone else to come, so you and Barb will have to do."

"Oh. Okay, I guess, but..."

"Just don't talk to anyone."

"Right."

As we drove in to Ullapool, Barb and I worried aloud about masquerading as something we're clearly not. When we arrived at the brightly lit Ceilidh Place hotel, Pete told the owner, Jean Urquhart, about our concern. She graciously waved it off. "This is quite informal – we only need a few tunes. Just join in when you feel you can. You won't need to mix with them. I'm sure they'll be pleased with whatever you can do."

When we came into the room, it was obvious that the travel writers had already been sampling the best of the Highlands. Pete unpacked his impressive array of instruments – guitar, mandolin, melodeon, pennywhistle – and took the floor with a smooth introduction that identified us simply as "my friends from Achiltibuie." From that near unpronounceable place name, the audience might have assumed that we were Gaelic speakers. In any case, no one seemed to think it odd that we spoke no English to them.

Pete started out by playing a few Highland airs, joyful and haunting music steeped in the local Gaeltacht tradition. Barb backed him with chords on her guitar, and I did my best to muffle the penetrating shrillness of my concertina. The travel writers listened dutifully to the unfamiliar tunes, but what they really wanted soon became clear when one man called out for 'Loch Lomond.' They all knew it, it was what they expected, and the enthused crowd joined in for the choruses.

For the remainder of our 'ceilidh,' Pete successfully drowned out my stumbling concertina with Scottish music-hall tunes, the sentimental sing-alongs popular with Americans, closing with the inevitable 'Auld Lang Syne.' At the end of an hour, the listeners were happy – due as much perhaps to the whisky as the music. The tour leader thanked Pete, we packed up our instruments, and headed back to Coigach. The American writers no doubt were left with fond memories of the genuine ceilidh they experienced that night, the wonderful 'Scottish' singer, and the two mute 'Highlanders' who played along.

As one who has traveled and toured myself, I'm sensitive to the expectations of people who travel far to experience the unfamiliar. Tourists hate to see other visitors intruding on their holiday fantasies. To avoid their glares when traveling around Britain, I try to disguise myself by wearing baggy tweeds and cloth caps and anything off the sale rack at Marks & Spencer. I have even attempted to walk with both hands clasped behind my back – a feat only the English have mastered. But to any European, my slouching posture, shambling gait and tendency to sprawl in chairs mark me indelibly as an American.

Still, in wellies and work clothes and lightly camouflaged with sheep shit, I can sometimes blend into the countryside and avoid disturbing the tourists who frequently stop on the road by Achnahaird fank to watch and take photos of us clipping sheep with traditional blades. It is a quaint and colorful Highland scene in which I – a counterfeit Highlander – usually try to keep a quiet, low profile. But one day temptation came along, and I gave in to it.

It was a bright warm day in high summer, and the usual crew was clipping: the Wests, Stookie, myself. Marilyn and Barb were rolling fleeces. Several cars had stopped, the passengers thrusting camera lenses through rolled-down windows. They seemed to think they were invisible, or that we were posed for their convenience like zebras in a safari park. Drive-by shooters they were, hoping to capture an exotic scene without risking contact with the native species. But one middle-aged man climbed out of his Ranger Rover and cautiously began to circle the fringe of the green.

He was small and slender and obviously shy – English by the look of him, tweedy jacket, tweedy cap, bow tie, large glasses framing wide eyes that gave him a bookish appearance. He held an expensive camera close to his chest, started to raise it a few times, but stopped, as a nature photographer might do to avoid spooking a wild creature. I began to realize that he was stalking me.

Almost on tiptoe he approached, awkward and hesitant. I continued clipping, a nice fat ewe with a good rise that made me look more adept than I was. For a while he crouched, motionless, on the periphery of my vision, then: "Ahem."

I ignored him and went on with my task.

"Excuse me..."

I looked up, wiping my brow with a shirt sleeve.

He clutched the camera halfway to his eye. "Um, I say – would you mind awfully if I took your picture?"

I thought for a moment before responding. "Well, you know," said I with my obvious Midwest American twang, "we natives believe that a photograph can take away a bit of our soul."

"Oh. Sorry."

"No, no, it's okay. Really. Go ahead and shoot."

Confused and embarrassed, the poor man snapped a shot off quickly and scuttled back to his car. In a moment he was gone. As were his illusions, no doubt.

## July 11th

*Another hot sunny day! Spent most of it doing ink drawings. Pete stopped by for tea and we went to visit Joan and Murdo this afternoon. It's been a while since we've seen them. Murdo looked pretty good. I think the warmth is good for him.*

*Went to the pub again last night and then to Ken the Bread's caravan for tea and a dram. He gave us a salmon that had been slightly damaged by seals – but so little that it made no difference to the meat. Lovely! We had a third of the salmon for supper tonight along with a big salad. Can't remember when I've had better – it was delicious.*

*A friend of Peter's has found us a first edition of Daniell's 1820 Tanera print and we sent off a check for it. Jack is all excited about it. I'll be glad to have it and yet I'm loath to buy anything – my joy in accumulating treasures is not what it was. The impermanence of our situation and lack of a home base makes me not want to possess anything but basic necessities. Jack and I are both feeling the passing of the time and our best days are tinged with sadness.*

*We still have no idea of what is possible in the future. Joan and Murdo keep hinting about us buying Castlehill and we don't know what to tell them. If Jack doesn't sell the book it will be a moot point. As for now – we'll get the most from each day as it comes.*

*Murdo said today (there was a bee buzzing around on the window) that his mother would always catch the first bumblebee of the season and put it in her purse because the saying was that if you did that your purse would always be full. He said that when she'd go to get money out as the year went on there'd be little pieces of wing falling out.*

Right now we're going about our bucolic Highland life, clipping sheep, rolling fleeces, living in a placid, timeless way. But we know we're floating in the quiet pool at the head of a tumbling rapids, and soon we'll be swept down among the rocks and wild spray and … even so, it beats just putting in your time and waiting for a gold watch.

We're already beginning to think – glumly – about leaving here, and all of the problems that will entail. We have no idea what our future will be, no idea when we will be back here. But we will be coming back, for certain. So – what do we bring back to the States, what do we leave behind? In some ways, the logistical hassles may be good – they'll take our minds off the difficulties of saying goodbye to the people here. Maybe. Dammit, I wish we were rich and could just flit back and forth between hither and yon – it would save a lot of emotional wear and tear.

## July 22nd

*We have had the most glorious weather lately. I'm sitting out here in the sun listening to the loudspeaker on the "Summer Queen" regaling the tourists with information on the islands they're passing. A trawler is steaming past – a really big one. The scallop divers are out – plus lots of fishing parties and quite a few sailboats. It's fun to see all the activity again.*

*Jack's clipping sheep at Achnahaird. I would be there but I've been baking and ironing and doing pen and ink drawings. This morning we went into Ullapool to copy the rest of his manuscript for an agent in the States who's interested. That's the second time this week. We got a call from another agent on Monday asking to see it. So now there are 4 full manuscripts out and we're getting quite hopeful that someone will like it enough to do something with it (other than send it back).*

*Monday this week we spent doing yard work – also Tuesday when we got back from Ullapool. Got the gates painted – they look nice. Tuesday evening it was so beautiful that we walked down to the Summer Isles for a pint and back. The sunset was spectacular behind the hills and everything was so clear – absolutely beautiful.*

*Wednesday we went to visit Joan and Murdo in the afternoon. We talked briefly about coming back and leaving some of our stuff here. Very little reaction actually – at least it doesn't look like they have any other plans for the house.*

*Last night we went into Ullapool with Pete and had fish and chips on the pier – yum! Pete and Jimmy were playing. The audience loved it – they were a real lively group and loved to sing. We left about midnight – the sky was a velvety blue fading into aqua with a hint of red and yellow around the edges. The moon on the sea and lochs was lovely.*

# Separated by a Common Language

There is an incomer here whose tongue has never forgotten his Glasgow origins. Glaswegians are notorious for their rapid, choked patois that strikes the ear something like "Guck th' huckhoo beck an' hick th' feckin hooly, eh, Jemmy?" Eddie's conversations always sound just like that to me. Apparently my neighbors can understand him, though, because Eddie loves to tell jokes at the pub, and everyone else finds him endlessly entertaining.

I tend to sidle away when Eddie is holding forth, as I would from a recitation in Bantu or Mandarin. No one wants to look like he just doesn't get it, and I usually didn't. Poor Barb, however, managed to get cornered between two others one day in the Fuaran when Eddie was holding forth, and he zeroed in on her.

"Heck th' mafoo gorn ta mucky, eh, hen?"

Barb nodded politely.

"So th' wee gackle smacked me gorble wakkerpad!"

She bobbed her head again, trying to look interested.

"Mickle furbin' slaw th' brimmin hobble, y'see?"

She raised her eyebrows noncommitally.

"Then th' wockle bandy higged th' miffer tae th' gack!"

Everyone roared. Barb joined in the mirth, attempting to look as if it were the funniest story she'd ever heard. When the laughter died down, the Glaswegian looked at her, grinned, and said – clear as a bell – "You didn't understand a word I said, did you?"

More laughter, but not from the red-faced American.

I had my own embarrassment the day I was introduced to Big Leslie's brother Rory. He had just returned from years spent working Down Under, where he had become seriously infected with a 'Strine accent. Trying to make small talk, I asked, "What were you doing in Australia?"

"Lye-brin," says he.

"Oh? Working with books, then?"

"Eh?" He frowned.

"You were a librarian?"

"Lye-brin," he repeated, very slowly, as if talking to a simpleton. "I was a lye-bor-er. You know," he gestured with both hands. "Workin' wi' a shovel!"

"Oh."

The first year I was clipping sheep at Achnahaird, a tourist stopped to watch us. He was a big man, with a craggy weathered face and calloused hands. After a while, he sidled over to the fank gate and, with a few muttered words and gestures, made clear that he wanted to help with the catching – which he did with considerable skill. It turned out he was a sheep farmer on holiday from the north of England, and he spent an hour of useful work with us.

When we took a tea break, he sat with us and struck up a long conversation with Alasdair. I couldn't comprehend his broad Northumbrian dialect, but assumed the two were talking sheep. When we went back to work, the man gave us a cheerful wave, said something unintelligible and drove away.

One fine day the following summer, the man returned to Achnahaird green. Again, he worked with us for an hour or so. Again he sat with Alasdair during a break, becoming quite animated in conversation. As he drove off, I turned to Alasdair. "What was all that about?"

"I haven't a clue," he replied. "I never understood a word he said!"

## July 24th

*So much has happened. Hmmm. We had tea with Joan & Murdo and she actually came right out and offered to sell us Castlehill if our ship comes in! If...*

*Wendy Stewart and Alan James and their friend Nick got here about 5:45. After dinner we went to the pub for a music session – then back here to play until 3:30 am. Jan and Peter from the hostel brought bass guitar and flute and recorders and we had a great evening of music.*

*This morning we got up and had a good hearty breakfast (about 11:00 am) and then wandered out on the lawn to sit in the bright sun with a brisk wind in the trees and listened to Wendy & Alan play. What a beautiful morning – the sound of the harp, sailboats among the islands and the wind in the leaves. The harp makes fairy music when the wind blows just right – an indescribably wonderful thing. Jack says " I would give a year of my life for a morning like this with the harp singing in the wind." The soul rejoices.*

*Joan stopped by and came up with Cap for a natter. (Cap was actually sweet and friendly – licked my face. I'm always afraid he's just tasting and will take a big bite any time!).*

*Jack's mother called – said air fares are going up on August 1, so we'd better get our tickets. Guess we'll have to go in to Inverness and see what we can find out.*

# Pride and Prejudice

The movie "Local Hero" was to the North of Scotland what "Ma And Pa Kettle" was to Appalachia, or "Li'l Abner" to the Ozarks: a caricature in half truths that says as much about the prejudices of the public as it does about the subject.

The Northwest Highlands have much in common with America's remote and mountainous regions. All are beautiful, mysterious, traditionally impoverished, and peopled according to popular mythology by backward, lazy, hard drinking locals. How do the locals in a place like Coigach feel about the outsiders who believe all this? You have to ask someone like Ali Post.

As you know, Post isn't Ali's real surname – it is a name he inherited the day he took up the wee red van and the fine blue gray uniform of Her Majesty's Royal Mail. Ali is a dark eyed, handsome young man, the oldest son of a family strong in the crofting tradition. He has a quiet, deliberate manner; but beneath is an active mind with typical Highland pride and a Highland sense of humor.

There was the unusually hot summer day when Ali and I set out to bury a dead ewe. The carcass had been discovered that morning at the back of a croft, already swollen and stinking in the sun. We leaned on our shovels upwind of her, looking hopelessly at the hard, rocky earth nearby. Then Ali looked off toward the grass topped sand dunes between the croft and a tourist camp on the beach below. "We'll bury her down there in the sand," he said. "It'll be easy digging."

"Won't the stink drive off the campers?" Even standing on the upwind side, I was gagging on the stench of her.

He smiled. "The wind'll keep it off for now, anyway."

We dragged the dead ewe down the hill. Noxious gases had ballooned the carcass to the point where we feared an explosion at every step. Nervous and sweating, we pushed it over the stone dike, and rolled it down to the side of the first dune. "This'll do fine," says Ali.

I looked over the top of the dune. A distinguished looking elderly Englishman sat reading a newspaper in front of his caravan, barely a hundred feet upwind. Beyond, dozens of tents, caravans and dormobiles were scattered among the dunes, and brightly clad tourists abounded like sand fleas, basking in the unaccustomed warmth of the day. "What if she bursts," I asked. "What if the wind shifts?" If the prevailing west wind were soon to prevail again, there would be a mass exodus from the beach campsite.

Ali said nothing, but he was grinning as he shoveled. It took him only a minute or two to scoop out a shallow hole. Then he stood back and nodded. "That'll be deep enough to cover her," he said with finality.

"Just barely," I said doubtfully.

"Aye." He looked toward the beach. A family was unpacking their picnic lunch; the Englishman had unbuttoned his shirt and exposed a fishbelly white chest to the sun. "Canny now," Ali muttered as we rolled the oozing, stinking carcass into the hole. "We don't want her to burst just yet."

We scooped sand over the corpse until it was buried like a land mine invisible, but an ever present danger to the unwary foot.

As we made our way back up the croft, we congratulated each other on how quickly and neatly we had disposed of the dead ewe. "You could bury a tourist like that," Ali said casually, "and no one would ever know."

"Oh, but you couldn't," I protested. "Someone for sure would report him missing."

"A tourist? No," he snorted. "There's millions of 'em."

Ali is very conscious of tourist notions about lazy, drunken Highlanders, and he reacts in a very Highland way. Like the time we had been working all morning to gather and sort new lambs to be docked, ringed and lug marked. Just as we were taking a much-needed break, two carloads of tourists came driving slowly past, their eager eyes taking in the quaint Highland scene. The lambs stood bawling in the pen, the ewes were baaaing outside the fence, and three of us in sheep-stained clothes were leaning on a drystone wall, passing a bottle of whisky.

"Oh gawd," I groaned, "we're just like a Highland stereotype."

"Let 'em think what they want," Ali snorted. He defiantly hoisted the bottle to his lips and pretended to take a long swig as the passing tourists stared.

The cars disappeared around a bend, and we went to work on the lambs.

It took us two hours of back breaking labor to finish the job, but at last we were done. Before we let the lambs out, Ali's father brought out the bottle and cups again for our second well earned break of the day.

And just at that moment, the same two carloads of tourists came back from their luncheon at the Summer Isles Hotel.

The scene they saw was apparently unchanged from two hours earlier.

The lambs still bawled inside the pen. The ewes baa-ed outside the fence.

And three of us were still leaning on the wall, passing the whisky bottle. As the wide-eyed tourists cruised past, Ali raised the still capped bottle in a casual salute to them before pretending to take a long, long swig...

## August 1st

*Windy, cool and cloudy today. Yesterday, however, was the most beautiful day of the summer – cool and crystal clear – a warm sun and the islands looked so close you could touch them. We spent all day from 9:30 – 7:30 clipping at West's. Jack took Murdo to the pub and then out to the fank. I drove him home through Altandhu and stayed for tea. A glorious day!*

*Met a chap at the pub this afternoon – told us the story about the Englishman who was translating Gaelic stories into English and asked Old Donald if there was a word in Gaelic that would be the same as the Spanish word "mañana." Old Donald thought and thought, then shook his head slowly and said "there is no word in Gaelic that conveys such a sense of urgency."*

# Autumn

༺❧༻

*September 4th*

*We're in the countdown for leaving. Anne & Iain and the Ali Beags came for dinner last night. Ali brought his accordion and we had a really good evening.*

*I went up in the hills on a gorgeous morning last week – up to Castle Rock and spent a few hours lying in the sunny heather looking out over the sea and islands – the hills purple now and the crofts soft and green. The rowan berries are red and the brambles ripening. I still feel that this is the most beautiful spot on earth – especially on sunny clear days – or when the clouds are hanging on the shoulders of the mountains and the sun spotlighting a ridge here and there.*

*Jack's gotten in a few more days of clipping and the dipping's all done. We went to the lamb sales in Dingwall on Thursday – a stunningly lovely day. It was a small sale – in fact it went so fast that John Alec missed the sale of his sheep entirely – he was in the social club at the time. The rest of them would have missed it too if Donnie hadn't checked in time. Everyone was through by 1:30 – way too early in the day. Prices were the same as last year – maybe even a bit lower. West got best price – £29.90 for top wethers. We all went over to the social club for lunch and a few games of pool – then to Ullapool and a pint in the Far Isles. It was a delightful day.*

*Today Murdo didn't go to the pub again – this is the third week now. He was taken sick while we were there – he hasn't been well at all – I really am worried about him now. He's not eating and looks terrible. I wish he'd go into Inverness for evaluation. But he's stubborn – he'll have to be on his last legs entirely before he'll go – if then.*

## September 7th

*Murdo died on Monday night. He had been failing for a while, hadn't been up to going out on our regular Saturday foray to the pub for about three weeks, and had been in quite a lot of pain for three days. He was still able to get about the house, though, and on Monday night he came down to listen to the evening news on the radio. About ten o'clock he went back upstairs, sat on the bed to undress, and keeled over.*

*Joan heard him fall, ran upstairs and found him dead on the floor. She called Wilf, and then the district nurse and the doctor. The doctor said it was either a stroke or a heart attack, but in any case it was instantaneous. Wilf stood by for a long time through the night, and called us the next morning. He has been a good friend to Murdo and Joan for years, and a mainstay at the moment.*

*We visited with Joan as much as possible and I brought her some food, as did other friends, so she had something to eat and feed the relatives who came for the funeral. Her minister came from Ullapool on Tuesday night to read scripture with her. But he is unhappy about having the funeral in the church here.*

*The funeral will be tomorrow afternoon.*

Murdo's coffin was placed inside the Achiltibuie Free Presbyterian Church – but it didn't get to stay there.

In Scotland, opinions are strongly held and so are grudges. Disagreements over theology, scriptural interpretation and doctrine – some fairly minor – have splintered the Scots Presbyterians into numerous stiffly exclusive sects: Church of Scotland, United Presbyterian Church of Scotland, Free Church of Scotland, United Free Church of Scotland – even 'Wee Frees' and 'Wee Wee Frees.' Their differences may seem largely incomprehensible to outsiders, but rigidly held as only Scots can hold them.

Joan and Murdo belonged to one such Presbyterian church, based in Ullapool, and the Achiltibuie church is of a different persuasion. Wilf said he was told that someone in the local congregation objected to the presence of a non-congregant corpse in the chapel. Whatever the truth of it, when we filed into the church for Murdo's last service, his coffin was left outside, alone, in the back end of a station wagon. In effect, poor Murdo was the only one in Coigach who didn't attend his funeral.

We sat through the short, impersonal service in the church, then followed everyone down to the little cemetery at Badenscallie. It's at the foot of the hill, just above the sea, with a good view of Loch Broom and the Dundonnell mountains across the way. You can see Tanera from there, where Murdo began his days, and the islands among which he rowed and sailed and worked for most of his life. It's a good place to think on him, too.

# A Farewell

I'm sitting alone on the sunlit hillside above the Badenscallie burial ground. I have just finished playing O'Carolan's 'A Farewell to Whisky' on my concertina, and for once the lovely air came out easy and gentle and I think Murdo would have enjoyed it.

Two years have passed since we left Minneapolis for the Highlands – two years of living in a way long forgotten by most people today, living close to the sky and the sea, the weather, the earth; living in an isolated, 'backward' community where people have time for each other and everyone is seen as an individual. It has been a wonderful time for us – but now it's over and we're leaving here.

The summer has been taken with music, as we have fallen in with quite a few traveling folk musicians who have spent long nights in our cottage. And I have been working with my friends and neighbors, taking care of their sheep. I am now considered a competent clipper with the blade shears, having clipped a few hundred sheep this summer, and Barb has become adept at rolling fleeces.

It's been quite a change for a couple of midwest American suburbanites, these days at the end of the Wee Mad Road, but we have fallen into the rhythms of the Highland world easily. Now, we're finding it difficult to leave, even though I look forward to returning to my own country again and my family and my friends.

These winding down days are painful and joyful together. Everything we do, every visit, every song, every day of work alongside our friends here, is haunted by the thought of impending loss. Something keeps getting in my eyes, and I'm rubbing them all too often. Still, I'm eager to return to America after two years' absence, and curious to see how it will seem to me through the filter of long separation.

# Afterward

## Ae Fond Kiss

Choices. Limitless choices. Barb and I sat on a bench in the atrium of a suburban Minneapolis shopping mall, awed by the bounty, the convenience, the whatever-you-want-here-it-is ambience. Having just come from a place where the need for one odd-sized bolt to fix the washing machine could mean a week's delay or a day's journey over the mountains and back, we looked at America's consumer world in a new light. Anything is easy to get, any time of the day or night. Restaurants, theaters, opera, zoos, museums, libraries, choices, choices, choices.

"Buy this, on sale now, ask your doctor about, have you seen..." Advertising hammered at us from signs and billboards and – worst of all – commercial TV and radio. But two years away from it all cured us of unthinking acceptance, made us unwilling to be subjected to the constant pitches. To this day, we avoid commercial TV, no longer listen to commercial radio. Life is nicer when you're not being hassled.

That first winter back, we house-sat for an acquaintance, watched the Minnesota snow deepen outside, re-connected our bonds with family and friends. My old customers welcomed me back, provided new script assignments and much-needed income. The technologies of their visual communication industry were changing from film to video, from reels to DVDs, and mine changed from typewriter to word processor (though I sometimes think the malevolent spirit of Benito lives on in computers today). It was an exciting time, and I was glad to be back for it. And glad to work closely again with producers, directors, cinematographers, film and sound editors, for writing fiction in Coigach was solitary work and I am by nature gregarious.

My freelance scripting assignments have taken me around the world while the manuscript for The Moccasin Bear, the novel I wrote in Coigach, languishes unread in a box in my closet. Publishers and agents are swamped with new fiction, and mine didn't win their attention. Part of the reason is my lack of marketing skill and perseverance. It's a good story, but I know it needs more work – and I haven't gotten around to doing it. New assignments, new challenges intervened. Life intervened. One of these days hasn't come yet. Yet.

We went back to Scotland the following April for Bill Baxter's wedding, then stayed on at Castlehill through the summer. But it wasn't the same. Coigach was already slipping into summer mode, the close community opening wide for tourists and everyone busy with visitors, including ourselves. There was little time for quiet evenings at home or small gatherings at the pub. And Murdo wasn't there.

We saw a lot of Joan, of course, and visited with other friends when they and we had time. Below the holiday surface of Coigach the gathering and dipping and clipping went on and we worked at it with Alasdair and Donnie and others through the summer. But now we were summer people ourselves, no longer a part of the small community that had weathered the winter months.

Another Fourth of July celebration, of course. And ceildhs and pub sessions. And days at the fishing, and picnicking on the islands, living out the last days of our Highland idyll. Castlehill was beyond reach, family and lifelong friends were proving a stronger magnet. It was clear to us now that soon it would be time to go home for good.

We said goodbye to Joan in September, promising to come back soon. For a visit. Not a stay. We said goodbye to our close friends in Coigach, and sang a last song with companions over the mountains as well.

*Ae fond kiss, and then we sever*
*Ae farewell, and then forever*
*Deep in heart-wrung tears I'll pledge thee,*
*Warring sighs and groans I'll wage thee.*

*Had we never loved sae kindly,*
*Had we never loved sae blindly,*
*Never met – nor never parted –*
*We had ne'er been broken-hearted.*

Although we returned to Coigach in the many years that followed, and kept up friendships to this day, it was never the same again. Young people became older, old people faded away, new waves of incomers took root and began their evolution into 'locals.' Old traditions tottered to the brink of extinction, then found renewal in devolved Scotland's Celtic renaissance; today the sons and daughters of the English-born study Gaelic in the Achiltibuie school.

A beautiful new community center has replaced the old Village Hall, which is now a piping school known throughout Scotland. The tunes Kenny John played on his fiddle, and songs sung in the old language by John Alec and Aggie and Hectoria and others of their time have been preserved on CDs, and the folklore of the region has been collected. What was taken for granted in the years we lived there – and almost lost to memory – has now been preserved in a new consciousness by a new generation.

The friendships we made were strong and lasting, but time has taken its toll. Donnie Darling, Alasdair West and John Alec no longer hold forth at the Fuaran. Wilf is gone, too, and Aggie, and others in Coigach who had generously made us welcome. Anne Irish and Iain have come twice to visit us in America, as have harper Wendy Stewart and Alan James. Others have kept in touch by letter through the years. One December day we received this note from the wife of Donnie Roll, or Donnie Post as we first knew him:

*Dear Barbara & Jack,*

*Just received your long letter & thank you for taking so much time to write. Yes, I remember well the days you describe & miss them also! It was nice that Joan died amongst her friends & that it was a sudden attack the same as Murdo.*

*Last summer I was telling her she would be 90 next birthday. She couldn't believe it & when I asked her what age she thought she was, she said "well, I knew I was 50 something."*

*I visited her two days before she died & re-read your last letter to her. She was remarking how mindful you both were of her always & how good you were to herself & Murdo. She was excited to hear that you were thinking of visiting the U.K. whenever – alas it was not to be that you meet again.*

*We thank God for her life – she was so outgoing & brought much sunshine into many lives. I will miss her as she was my favourite Auntie as was Murdo my favourite Uncle.*

*Yours aye, Hilary*

As for us? Some things changed, some stayed the same. Barb, at age 46, went back to school for two years, then started an entirely new professional career. I returned to what I had been doing before – the only difference being that I now know writing scripts is my choice, not just a living by default. To me, that discovery alone made it worth the journey.

We had lived without demands on our time for a while, but it couldn't last. In the following years, aging parents, marrying daughters, the advent of a grandson required our attention. Opportunities and responsibilities came along. And suddenly we are here in the now, still together, still looking for adventure.

We took to The Wee Mad Road one day, and followed it to its end. But a road once traveled can never be new again. Perhaps, just around the next corner, another wee mad road begins – and the best roads are the ones that surprise you.

*Visit Coigach and drive The Wee Mad Road with us at:*

*www.theweemadroad.com*

# Acknowledgements

Every book is shaped by people whose names don't appear on the cover. <u>The Wee Mad Road</u> would never have been written without the persistent urging of Robin and Jean Sinclair of Shetland and Saint Paul. Their first visit to us in Castlehill was the foundation of an enduring friendship.

Donn Larson of Duluth, a valued colleague throughout my writing years, edited the manuscript at his summer home in Cloud Bay, Ontario. He and his wife, Donna, helped us avoid more than a few hazards on the journey.

Photographer Steve Niedorf, with whom we have paddled, backpacked, skied and climbed in many a natural wilderness, made digital copies of Barb's illustrations and provided invaluable guidance through the wilderness of technology.

To them, to our family and friends who stayed true in our absence, and especially to all those who made us welcome at the end of The Wee Mad Road: may all your roads be as joyful. Slainte mhath. Slainte mhor!

# Place Names

*That Elusive Gaelic 'CH' Sound*

The 'ch' sound in Gaelic place names is tricky for English-speakers. It is not a hard 'k,' nor yet a 'ch' as in 'itch.' It is a soft, aspirated sound, sort of an 'h' with the back of your tongue almost against the back of your palate. It's much like the 'ch' in German ich, or 'kh' in Arabic khalid. If you just give up and make it a hard 'k,' you'll be forgiven. And even if you get it right, they'll still know you aren't a local.

**Achiltibuie** -ACH-ilty-BOO-ee

**Achnahaird** – ACH-na-haird

**Achduart** – ach-DOO-art

**Altandhu** – allt-an-DOO

**An Teallach** – an-TCHA-lach

**Coigach** – KOY-gach (the 'g' is barely heard, so it almost sounds like KOY-ach)

**Culnacraig** – KOOL-na-krayg

**Dirrie Mor** – jirry MOR

**Drumrunie** – drum-ROO-nee

**Drumbeg** – drum-BEG

**Eilean a Char** – AY-lan-a-CHAR

**Fuaran** – FOO-ran

**Glas Leac** – GLAHS-lick

**Polbain** – pole-BAIN

**Strathkanaird** – strath-KAN-yard

**Suilven** – SOOL-ven

**Stac Pollaidh** – stack-POLL-y

**Tanera** – TAN-era

# Glossary

<blockquote>

## Sheep Terms

**gimmer** – a lamb in its second year,
        sort of a teenager
**hogg** – a lamb in its first year, still a child
**tup** – ram (male sheep) used for breeding
**wether** – castrated male sheep
**yow** – ewe

</blockquote>

**beag, beg** – Gaelic: small or little
**blade**s – steel scissor-like hand instrument used for clipping sheep
**blow** (clipping) – one full cut of the blades
**bodach** – old man
**bothy** – shelter, small cottage or bunkhouse for workers
**buist** – (byoost) paint mark used for color-coding sheep
**burn** – small stream
**ceilidh** – (KAY-lee) an evening's entertainment, usually informal,
        often spontaneous
**clootie dumpling** – a spicy, fruit-filled pudding boiled in a cloth
        (clootie) and warmed at the fireside
**come by!** – tells dog to circle sheep clockwise
**clipping** – using blades to take off a fleece
**coble** – a small work boat designed to be hauled up on a beach
**crack** – lively conversation
**dike, drystane dike** – a wall between fields, built of local stones,
        without mortar
**dipping** – semi-annual chemical bath to protect sheep from
        insects and fungus
**dram** – a small glass of whisky (sometimes not small)
**fank** – a set of pens used for sorting sheep into separate groups
**fleece** – the wool clipped or sheared from a sheep, held together
        by its own fibers

**get out!** – tells dog to get away from sheep

**jagging** – using a hypodermic needle to administer medication

**knackered** – exhausted

**mor, more** – Gaelic: big, grand

**nattering** – chatting

**publican** – pub owner

**rise** – natural separation of the fleece from a sheep's skin as new growth pushes away last year's wool

**shearing** – mostly refers to using motor-driven shears to take off a fleece

**slainte mhath** – (SLAN-tcha VA) Gaelic toast: to your good health!

**slainte mhor** – (SLAN-tcha VOR) response: to your great health!

**steading** – a small barn

**VAT** – value added tax

**walk up!** – tells dog to move toward sheep

**way to me!** – tells dog to circle sheep counterclockwise